corked

A MEMOIR

k a t h r y n   b o r e l

GRAND CENTRAL
PUBLISHING

New York   Boston

Grand Central Publishing
Hachette Book Group
237 Park Avenue
New York, NY 10017

www.HachetteBookGroup.com

Printed in the United States of America

First Edition: February 2010
10 9 8 7 6 5 4 3 2 1

Grateful acknowledgment is made to reprint from "If I Had a Boat," written by Lyle Lovett. © Michael H. Goldsen, Inc./Lyle Lovett. Used by permission.

Grand Central Publishing is a division of Hachette Book Group, Inc.
The Grand Central Publishing name and logo is a trademark of Hachette Book Group, Inc.

Library of Congress Cataloging-in-Publication Data
Borel, Kathryn.
  Corked: a memoir / Kathryn Borel.—1st ed.
    p. cm.
  ISBN 978-0-446-40950-6
  1. Borel, Kathryn. 2. Borel, Kathryn—Travel—France. 3. Fathers and daughters. 4. Wine tourism—France. 5. France—Description and travel. I. Title.
  CT275.B5845195A3 2010
  914.404092'2—dc22   2009017207

Illustrations by Cody Cochrane
Book design by Giorgetta Bell McRee

For my family

acknowledgments

I am grateful for the guidance, generosity, kindness, and support of the following people: Leah Fairbank, Emily Griffin, Sam Hiyate, Amy Einhorn, Lindsay Humphreys, Rémy Gresser, Manou Massenez, Alex Heinrich, Bernard Nast, Marie-Anne and Jean-René Nudant, René Aubert, Chantal Comte, Pierre Larretche, Jean-Noel Bousquet, Anne-Marie and Roland Coustal, Christine Simon, Peter Armstrong, Andy Barrie, Abigail Brodovitch, Amy Cameron, Cody Cochrane, Benson Cowan, Jeremy Gans, Richard Green, Sheila Heti, Barry Isaacson, Chuck Jutras, Ibi Kaslik, Sisley Killam, Su Lin Lewis, Matthew Pemberton, Adrienne Reid, John Rowley, Julia Rosenberg, David Stevenson, Bill Stunt, Michel Busch, Kyle Buckley, and the entire team at CBC Radio One's Q.

I am most indebted to Philippe Borel, Kathryn Borel Sr., and Nicolas Borel. Without you, I would be a broken egg on the sidewalk.

corked

chapter one

When it comes to champagne and our family, my father has only one absolute rule: We do not drink it when we are sad.

In the pebbled courtyard of this audaciously French bed-and-breakfast, my father and I stretch our limbs. His arms flap out, parallel to the expanse of pigeon gray pebbles, his palms wide and splayed, as though he's holding the most gigantic pair of hedge clippers and is just about to cut a bush into a topiary of a cock. The rooster kind. He flings his arms as wide as they'll go, pulsing them over and over. As he flings, he spits out a sequence of vowels found in Dutch words: "OO!" "EE!" "AA!" . . . "OO!" "EE!" "AAAAA!"

I drop my head to my knees and hang there, feeling the xylophone click of my vertebrae, smelling the wind that bursts around us. It's fresh and animated, loaded with invisible particles that blow off the clusters of fruit from the vineyards surrounding the B&B. The vineyards go on and on, interminable grids of interminable rows of interminable vines. The stone house looks besieged by the vines, as if it could, at any moment, be overtaken by these squat, spiky plants should they decide to uproot themselves, devise a plan, walk the short distance, and begin a good old rampage of vine-thrashing destruction.

Pressing out the last bit of air from the bottom of my lungs, I pop up and jog over to my father, punching the air with each step. When I arrive at his puffed chest, I reach out my hand, which I've formed into a claw, and pantomime tearing out his heart. I hold the heart in one hand, turn around, and drop-kick it into the nearest field, which is now turning all iris and gold as the big country sky shuts down for the day.

"Thank you, Tou Tou. I didn't need that old thing anyway," he says. Tou Tou is my French nickname. It is slang for "baby dog."

"Suze-la-Rousse." I say the name of the town we're in like a proclamation.

"Suce la rousse," my father mispronounces on purpose.

"Suck the redhead," I translate.

"Yesssss! I've done this many times." Maybe he is making a joke.

"Gross. Suck the redhead. Gross." But I laugh, because we've just come from a terrific wine tasting in the glorious Rhône Valley, in the vineyards of Châteauneuf-du-Pape.

The owner's wines tasted of delicious cake, and in his relaxed southern French manner, he'd opened more than a dozen bottles for us to sample. I couldn't bear to spit any of them out, so I swallowed and swallowed each sip of delicious cakey wine. Now, with all this new gulped air and the remains of the booze, I have become a little drunk again. My father shouldn't have allowed me to drive. I shouldn't have allowed me to drive.

When we rap on the glass door of the stone house, a small pit-bullish woman greets us. She is in her early thirties and has a wide-eyed, moon-faced baby perched on her hip. She allows us to take two steps into the front room, then blocks our passage. Immediately, she sniffs out my accent.

"Americans?" she asks in English. Her accent is convincing. This is a shock to vaguely drunken me, considering her house is in a tiny village and she's surrounded by more plants than people.

"Canadian, actually," I respond in English. "But my father, here, is French. French from France. This France, here." I point twice at the ground, to show her what France I am talking about. "Paris." I point up, where Paris lives.

"Oh." She seems disappointed. "I used to work in America. I was a catering manager for a hotel in Washington, D.C." She says this fast; she seems ravenous for conversation.

"That's what my father does. He's a hotelier." My father momentarily takes his attention away from wagging his index finger in front of the baby's face and nods to corroborate my statement. He immediately goes back to the baby, letting his finger slice through the air slowly. Left and right, left and right. He looks like a cop administering a sobriety test to a tiny impaired driver.

"I admire the American work ethic. I want to go back there. Do you know the French unions are petitioning for even *shorter* weeks? Thirty-one and a half hours. It's lazy. I can't stand it. But my husband is based here. That's why we opened the B and B. I want to leave this shithole," she sputters.

I do a slow 180-degree turn to gaze out her door. Magic hour is in full, foolhardy effect, frosting the gnarly vines with platinum. Bars of golden light poke through the surrounding tree branches, most still covered with leaves the color of cartoon fire. Startled by something we do not see, a beige cluster of birds explodes skyward. I turn back and examine the interior of her home: the thick, gray brown high beams, the exposed stone walls, the smooth octagon terracotta tiles, the wide bay windows bracketed by fresh linen curtains, sheer and bright.

"I see what you mean," I respond. I reach out my hand for the keys and tap my fingers gently to my thumb. She rests them in my palm and tells us where our rooms are.

We thank her, exit, and walk along the grass path that leads to a row of individual coach houses. We dump our bags in our neighboring rooms and cross-inspect each other's living arrangements. We both have stone terraces and delicate wrought-iron tables outside. Inside, four-poster beds and mosquito nets, large bathrooms with clean porcelain and clawed tubs.

"Dad, she's right, this place is a real shithole."

"Toots, let's go out and celebrate *zees* shithole town and our shithole trip," he says. "We'll have some nice dinner, some nice champagne."

After I splash a quart of freezing water on my face and resurrect, fifty times, the lost art of the jumping jack—for sobriety's sake—we climb back into our rented Citroën Picasso and trek south to a restaurant in Châteauneuf. My dad has a nebulous memory of an unforgettable meal he had there once, several years ago, on another wine trip with my mother, Kathryn Borel Sr. Her nickname is Blondie, because of her hair. That was also the name of Hitler's dog, though my father claims these things are unrelated.

"*Eet* was truly memorable," he says as we pass the white sign that confirms we are in the correct town.

"Which way?"

"I can't remember."

"Should I go in the direction of the *centre-ville*?"

"Why not." He is distracted by something again. Earlier in the day, he had a bizarre moment in the car, before we were about to meet the vineyard owner at Châteauneuf-du-Pape. He sat there, sullen and impenetrable, inhaling through his front teeth as if he were about to say something. When I reached out to touch him near the little rogue hairs next to his left eyebrow, he swatted my hand away without kindness. I placed both hands on my knees and stared at them until the owner of the wine house, René Aubert, an arachnid man, all spindly legs and arms, burst into the courtyard.

"Is this ringing any bells?"

"Not yet," he says.

I wait a beat. "What about now?" I make a joke, hoping it will lift this new strange mood that's in the car.

"No siree," he says in a quiet voice.

We pass some trees. The sun has set, and their branches are ugly in the dark.

"Now?"

"Okay, Toots. Enough." He reaches over and pats my knee. I glance over at him. He blinks heavily.

I focus on being a good driver for him. Smooth and calm, no jerky turns or hard brake pumps. Maybe he is just hungry and tired. Also, his bum knee was acting up today. Sixty-six-year-olds with bum knees become cranky when they are not fed on time. The goal is champagne; our night will be happy.

"Oh!" he exclaims.

"Something familiar?"

"No. I forgot my *bréviaire*." For the last thirty years, his dining ritual has been to make tasting notes on all the wines he selects and drinks. He scrawls them in his illegible chicken scratch in his leather-bound Day-Timer. But napkins and coasters are always an option for those scribbles. He is being difficult.

"Dad. Listen. I brought my desk calendar, if you need to make notes. Help me out here. Can you at least tell me where to park?" There are street spots available, but our car won't fit into them.

He ignores me and goes back to focusing on something else, so I settle on a parking lot at the bottom of a hill that leads up to where I surmise the restaurant will be. Getting out of the car and looking at the slope up ahead, I immediately know he's going to complain about the walk. I wonder if I'm trying to provoke a reaction.

"But Tootsie, the hill. My knee. My poor knee!" I ball up my hands into fists, squeeze, and release. He whines like a child.

"We can take the hill slowly, Dad. Okay? There was nowhere to park up there. I. Will. Help. You."

"Thank you. Thank you, Tootsie." Three glasses of champagne pop into my head, bowing to me, then to one another, before lining up in front of my grabby hands. I imagine draining the trio in rapid sequence and hiccuping merrily. Problem? There is no problem. Problems are for those who lack champagne.

It takes fifteen minutes for my gimp to shuffle his way up the hill and into the town square. Each of the four sides is quaint. In the middle is a fountain. Surrounding it are two bistros, one bar and one restaurant. Faint music and lights pour out of each.

"So. Daddy. Which one is it?" I ask. I am careful about making my tone even. Maybe he is mad or sad or tired or hungry or some emotion I've never heard of.

"Hmm." He turns around and around—a dog chasing his tail in extreme slow motion.

"Dad, I don't want to rush you, because I am eager to eat a memorable meal at this memorable restaurant. But I am also very—" I stop myself before I say the word *hungry,* because I am worried that my needs will make him annoyed.

"Yes, yes, Toots. I think it is . . . eh . . . this one."

"La Garderie."

"Yes. But I can't remember for sure," he says dismissively, withdrawn. He feels like a bomb or a snail.

"Great, then. Good enough."

We enter, there is a bar. We stand in front of the bar, waiting to be seated in the dining room next door. Waiters come and go, making drinks behind the bar and carrying them to tables, not acknowledging us. My dad lets out a sigh. If only this sigh were louder and were accompanied by a translator or a Geiger counter. Our family would have avoided countless hospitality disasters if a person or little machine had begun screaming toxicity reports at the staff. These nights always, always, ALWAYS begin with a sigh, and, if the crappy status quo is maintained, always, always, ALWAYS end with my dad's invective equivalent of Mount Vesuvius. Too many times I've watched him grow chilly and dismissive with a waiter for accidentally bringing wine from the wrong year, or blast the food and beverage manager of a hotel for allowing any soft triple-cream cheese, like Brie or Camembert, onto a complimentary cheese platter set in my dad's room as a VIP gift. (Soft triple-cream cheeses stink up the room. Hard cheeses are acceptable.) There's a minefield element to traveling with my father. "I love making people feel like *sheet* about themselves," he says. "I would like to teach a university course in this." My father's boundaries are elliptical, and though they're impossible to predict, stepping over them is an exercise in arbitrary terror. It would take a team of good Jungian men to properly navigate them. Stepping outside the line is usually fine. And other times, you get your face and limbs blasted off.

I turn toward my father and tug on the sleeve of his navy blazer. He has cleaned himself up for our champagne dinner—his peppery gray hair is elegantly combed back, his smooth tan face is brown as nuts and softly moisturized. His once full mouth now droops a bit from age, but it remains firm above a strong jaw and tall neck. He is a fine gentleman, a movie star from the 1950s or 1973.

"Dad. Please. Please please please. We'll be seated, I'm sure of it. They have to seat us! It's the way these things work. It took us a while to get here, three more minutes will not be the end of the world," I say, knowing full well that three more minutes could, in fact, be the end of the world.

"Tootsie, you're right. This is a night of celebration," he says.

I sigh a sigh of relief.

A young waitress wearing a great deal of gold eyeliner sways over to us. *"Vous voulez manger?"*

Would we like to eat? Yes, we would. My father takes in a quick breath and straightens himself so that he's at his maximum towering height. Before he can say, "Well, what the fuck else would we be here for, *connasse?*" I grin and respond, *"Avec plaisir."*

She leads us to a prettily dressed white table with a little candle. Upon returning to the back section of the restaurant, she begins to joke with another waiter, a hot, chiseled man with a hairdo like the wig of a Lego figurine. My father watches her, unblinking. The temperature in my earlobes shoots up as I crane my neck around to see if she's making appropriate serving progress. I feel a fleeting warmth in my chest and bathing suit area for the hot waiter, but I'm too worried to indulge in the abandon of server-lust fantasies. Maybe I think about him sucking on my wine-stained lower lip for one-half of one second, but I'm really just praying silently and laser-focused on the pile of untouched wine lists.

Oh Christ. The wine list. Bring us one copy of the wine list, bar wench. You're standing right by the goddamn stack. Seriously. That's all we need to fix this, to put this night back on the rails. The tiniest of tweaks . . . and we're back! Right there on the rails, where we should be. Girl, if you want to walk away from tonight with your life and your pride, you'd best bring us the wine list, you skinny 1970s-knockoff teenager.

I look at my father—whose eyes are morphing into flamethrowers—and feel the great heat descend from my earlobes down into the rest of me. It is not the good kind of heat.

Perhaps I'll just scoot over there and fetch the wine list myself! No, no. That's gauche, and will only anger him more. She'll bring it. I have faith. No, I don't. She's going to grow wings specifically so that she can pluck a feather and make a quill, and she will stab the quill into her own wrist and write an erotic poem of Homeric proportions in her blood. Wine list? The only feasible prospect of her bringing us the wine list is if she hits a main artery and needs my napkin to make a compress wound dressing.

Doubling over, she laughs at something the Lego man says and coyly puts her hand on his shoulder to right herself.

My dad raises his hand. I intervene before he can say anything disgraceful.

"Dad, please, when she comes over here, just ask her for the wine list. Please don't ruin the evening. Please don't say anything that will piss her off. Please. Please promise me. Do it right now. Say, 'I promise.'" My stomach is feeble.

"Okay, Toots. Relax. I promise." The words come out with no pauses in between. No pauses means no promises. I am not a fucking dummy. There will be no champagne tonight.

"No. Dad. Look at me and say you promise."

He glances at me and waves his raised hand once, casually. *"Excusez-moi, mademoiselle,"* he says just a tiny bit too loudly. The other diners turn to look at the disturbance. With heroic lethargy, she walks over to the table. I look closely at her face. Under all the paint and defiance, there's the face of a girl. She's eighteen, maybe.

My father drums his fingers three times on the tablecloth and squints. That is it. A wave of premature hurt ripples through me.

"So," my father begins, "how would you like to proceed, mademoiselle? Would you like me to tell you how to do your godforsaken job, or are you so stupid I should simply do it for you?"

"Pardon?" she says. Her tone is deliberately offhand. Looking up at her briefly, I see that she is smirking, but with the wobbly mouth of a child. I fixate on the candle again.

"Obviously, my being here is a massive imposition, and your establishment magically keeps itself afloat by treating its patrons like dog shit, am I correct?" My dad raises his voice by several decibels.

"Well, sir . . ."

Everyone who is eating has put down their cutlery. Everyone on staff has stopped in their tracks. All eyes are on us: table dystopia. The Lego waiter's face is grim. A couple sitting at the table behind my father's chair have their heads down. The woman mutters *"S'il vous plaît."* I think I hear her husband call my father an ass.

He goes on, arms flagging.

"Well, sir what? WELL, SIR WHAT? DO YOU NEED TRAINING? DO YOU WANT ME TO BE YOUR TRAINER? WHEN TWO PEOPLE WALK INTO A RESTAURANT YOU DO NOT DISAPPEAR YOU BRING THEM THE WINE LIST SO THEY CAN HAVE A DRINK. THERE, THAT IS YOUR TRAINING. BUT WHAT I WILL NOT DO IS SIT HERE AND PAY MONEY OUT OF MY WALLET WHILE I TRAIN YOU TO DO YOUR FUCKING JOB."

I reach for my jacket and stammer, "Dad. Please just let's go." The room is swimming, cloudy. It is as though my eyeballs have been dipped in Vaseline.

He is still yelling as he rips his blazer off the chair, knocking it over.

The waitress says, "You're welcome to eat somewhere else, sir." In her hands is the wine list. She drops it accidentally. I pick it up and hand it to her, staring at her belt because I don't want to look at her face. She thanks me in a small voice.

My father storms through the restaurant, passing every table. I follow, wishing myself dead. Couples quickly cast their eyes down and stare at their plates. Two teens, eating with their parents, are muffling laughter.

When we get to the door, my father grabs the handle and jostles it. It is locked. Naturally. Why wouldn't it be locked? He jostles and jostles. God. Why. Why more of this? I know people are watching, and this causes jolts of pain to fire through my neck. Seriously. We have to get the fuck out. He has to get the fuck out of my way. His rage is obliterating his motor skills.

"Dad, let me get it," I whisper. He moves to the side; I unhinge the door. We burst out into the cool evening air and I drink it in heaves. All is quiet; the wind from earlier has disappeared. Merry music continues to wander out from the other restaurants, the wide sounds cheerfully distorted, into the twinkly blue night.

I look up at him. Hot tears are pooling faster than they

can splash out my eyes and it makes him blurry, as though I am seeing a reflection in a lake.

I want to scream, "What the fuck is the matter with you?" But I can't. I am afraid. I am afraid that he could turn his anger on me. He could just shoot me full of holes with it. Instead, I regress; I can practically feel it happening in my body. It feels like all my insides are being sucked up. I need to get mad at him, but I need him to stay with me. So like a little child I shout, "YOU PROMISED."

"But Tootsie, I was right. She was wrong."

"It doesn't matter who was right or wrong. What matters is YOU PROMISED. YOU PROMISED ME. REMEMBER ME?" I yell these words as loud as I can, thinking for a moment that my volume will make up for their uselessness. It doesn't work. Not even close.

I storm off. I don't bother to check if he is following. I can hear his clip-clopping gait behind me. He is trying to catch up, but his knee is slowing him down. His poor, poor knee. Well, fuck his knee. I speed up and set off down the hill to the parking lot.

"Tootsie!" His voice is far away. "Wait!"

I break into a faster walk, almost a jog, then a pumping sprint, until I reach the Citroën. It is sitting shadowy and forlorn in the parking lot. Still sobbing, I turn on the ignition and jam the transmission into first, flooring the accelerator until the engine screams like a chainsaw. *"I'VE ENDURED AND COMPENSATED FOR A LIFETIME OF THIS FUCK-SHIT BEHAVIOR."* I bellow this to myself. I spin around and out of the lot, swerving toward his hobbling figure, which is not even halfway down the hill. The lights flash on him and he cowers a little. I whale on the horn. A thought skitters through my head, like a disoriented chipmunk darting out of a bush. For one searing flash of a moment, I think it would be a very funny joke if I were to hit him.

chapter two

Two weeks earlier, my father and I were dancing cheek to cheek.

We were in the presidential suite of the Queen Elizabeth Hotel in Montreal, on the eve of our wine odyssey, and we were joke-dancing across the freshly vacuumed taupe carpet as if we were in a village idiot's version of a Fred Astaire film. When my father dances, he notches up his alto voice to a warbling soprano and in a halfhearted, mumbling singsong croons things like "Ehhh . . . eeee . . . we are danciiiiing . . . Here we are . . . danc*eeeee*ng . . . da da da . . . do do do . . . cha cha cha . . . *danciiiiing* . . ."

Our cheeks were smushed together indelicately, like two old, forgotten oranges shoved in the toe of a Christmas stocking. My hand was on his shoulder, his hand on my waist. His right arm and my left one stuck straight out and were connected at the knuckles. We were a clumsy watering can, shuffling and hopping around the spent room service cart with its leftover Caesar salad smells; we mumbled his da-da-da-dancing song, our voices screeching higher and higher as we tried to contain the laughs simmering in our guts.

"Okay. Enough!" My father let go of my hand.

"Thank you for the dance," I said, doubling over in a splendid ceremonial bow.

"No, thank *you* for the dance," he responded, bowing lower.

"No, thank *YOU* for the dance," I shouted, leaning into the bow until I fell slowly onto my shoulder. I lay there, seizing in and out of my now horizontal bow—a grateful epileptic.

Cackling, my father helped me up. I walked over to the darker taupe couch and began drawing a two-slice toaster on a pad of hotel stationery.

"Tootsie. Don't mess around. Look at *zees*. Read it to me out loud." He threw a thin bound document at my head. It hit me in the face and dropped onto my lap. At the top of the cover page, under a cover sheet of plastic, were the words *Safari Vinicole en Terre de France*. Our itinerary. Picking it up, I noticed the many pages inside.

"You really stacked this trip, huh, Dad," I said.

"Start reading, Toots," he ordered. He'd gone back to the Caesar salads and was running a crouton along the square ivory plate, ineffectively using the thing to collect smears of dressing.

"Monday, September twenty-sixth." I read the date at the top of the page using the fake Cronkite-style broadcast voice I'd assumed while goofing around during rehearsal newscasts in the radio studio of my journalism school.

"Not the *dates*, Tootsie. The places."

"Paris, then Contrexéville . . ."

"They make water there. It's next to Vittel. There, they also make water. We will baptize ourselves with water before we become soaked with wine." He sounded like a preacher, even though he is an atheist.

"Good news," I said.

"It will take three hours to get there," he announced.

"Then we spend the night in Contrexéville, then we go to Alsace . . ."

"Which will take another three hours." He nodded, affirming his knowledge of his homeland's geography.

"The next day, we have three meetings. Rémy Gresser, Manou Massenez, and Alex Heinrich." I looked up from the page and saw that my father was pretending to sleep, chin on chest. Feeling my gaze, he pursed his lips to generate drool. I went on.

"The next day, we are going to the Alsatian baby donkey farm to buy a dozen baby donkeys, each of whom I will name after one step in the Alcoholics Anonymous program."

"Okay. Sorry. I'm back." He opened his eyes wide and shot me an openmouthed grin, as if he were coming out of the most restful hypnotic trance.

"We have a tasting at Clos Isenbourg, with Alex Heinrich's

sommelier." I paused to think. I realized I knew nothing about Alsace. Flipping madly through my memory's Rolodex, ripping out cards, throwing them on the floor, I willed myself back to his wine cellar in New Jersey, where we'd lived when I was small. We lived in a house, yes, but on the weekends I was forced to live in the cellar, my father's cellar. The cellar in which I'd stand, feet freezing, nose choking on clammy air, loving my father as equally as I hated that cellar and the oenological lessons he was so pathological about imposing on me there.

Suddenly, in a fit of synesthesia, I remembered something. Alsace has green bottles.

"Go on," he urged.

"Alsace has green bottles," I said.

"Uh, yes, my Tou Tou."

For my entire young adulthood, I'd been pretending. Pretending at most things, but pretending a *lot* in matters concerning wine. He believes these facts he has taught me are latent. I am relatively certain they've been sucked into a parallel dimension. There live my childhood wine lessons, in the same universe as all our lost single socks. And the Krugerand my great-grandmother gave me when I was eight.

"Tell me something about Alsace," I said.

"You know about Alsace."

"Yes, I do. It has green bottles. Refresh my memory with some other stuff. Please, Dad."

"Alsace . . ." He sighed and scanned his own memory banks for a comestible sound bite for me. "In Alsace, we will drink the highest expression of the Riesling grape. We will be in Colmar, in the north, where they make very different Riesling wines from the ones from the south. You will taste purity. *La minéralité.* Why Alsace? The lovely flowery little villages. The mountains. The confluence of two historical pillars of Europe, France and Germany, that are united, in a way, because of wine."

"Oh, lovely. And we will eat sausage and cheese," I stated.

"We sure will," he said.

Satisfied, I continued reading. "Then we drive to Burgundy."

"Which will take many hours," he said, drawing out the "a" in "many," to alert me of how very many hours it would take.

"Then it's more vineyard visits and tastings. The domaine of François Lamarche in Vosne-Romanée. After lunch, the domaine of the Nudant family. And then we drive to the Rhône Valley."

"Oh, so many hours, my Tootsie!"

I flipped to the back of the book and found color printouts of French maps, with some brief driving instructions. I tallied up the kilometers to a number well over one thousand. I looked up at my father again. He had abandoned his croutons and was grimacing as he jabbed one of his omnipresent used pocket toothpicks around his teeth.

"Now tell me something about Burgundy!" I demanded, wanting the information less than I wanted to see him put the wet stick back into his shorts pocket.

"Burgundy is too complex for a little story. You are a Burgundy," he said.

"Okay. Fine. Tell me something about Côtes-du-Rhône, then," I said.

"Here's a story for you, Tou Tou. In 1972, I was in the Rhône Valley. *Eet* was a vacation. *Eet* was the site of my very first private wine tasting. Things were going well for me, finally, after a very bad time." He stopped and thought a bit about this.

"What was the bad time?" I asked.

"Forget it. *Ce n'a pas d'importance*," he said. I wanted to push him, but his face was drawn and he seemed annoyed by the memory. And I didn't want to hear him say the words, "Can I finish my story?" My father can orate for hours on end. When I was younger, I would grow bored and interrupt him. He'd raise his voice, not in volume but in octaves, and say, "Can I finish my story?" This would make me feel like an idiot. I'd rather be bored than feel like an idiot.

He continued, "I was the new vice president of Skyline Hotels. I had good clothes, nice things. It was my first return to France in many years. It felt like a homecoming. I arrived in Châteauneuf-du-Pape in the evening, after driving from the north. In the town, I was walking around. I came across a big old farmhouse with a big chimney. It belonged to a couple of cousins who were known in the town. Young men. They were called Fabre-Abeille."

"What were their first names?" I sounded interested. I was interested.

"I can't remember. Don't interrupt. This is a good story. I am telling you something good. So I walked into this open farmhouse. It was attached to a vineyard, and it was clear I could sample the wines they were making. They were friendly folks, country folks, who had just taken back the family's vineyards from their fathers and were trying to launch their wines. They told me to sit, and for the next couple of hours, they ran back and forth, getting new bottles of wine, opening them, and sampling them with me. They opened ten bottles, probably. We did a lovely *dégustation*. They brought me cheeses, meats, some fresh country bread. By the end of the evening, I walked out of their operation with a couple of bottles of wine, and went back to my hotel. I had a big fight with the woman who ran the hotel . . ."

"Your fault," I said.

"Her fault," he said.

"Of course."

"I took my bottles of wine and went into the town square. It was dark and late. I sat on the steps and opened one bottle. As I was drinking it, I noticed there were two *clochards* . . ."

"Hobos . . ."

"Right, *hobos*, sitting on a bench across the little square. They were staring at me, at my wine, at my bounty. It was getting a little cold out, it was October. The air was chilly. I asked them if they had any kinds of cups or glasses. They both said they did. So I walked over to them, poured my wine into their cups, and we all toasted to friendship, to hope. No one cried, but everyone's eyes were a bit shiny. When I went back to the hotel, I smoked my pipe and thought, *We are all des hommes de bonne volonté,*" he said, quoting the title of the Jules Romains series he used to make me read out loud to him in New Jersey, after my wine lessons. He'd wanted to make sure my French didn't find itself in the universe of lost socks.

"Tha—"

"I'm not finished. Thirty years later—we're talking 2002 now—Blondie and I take a trip around France. We find ourselves in Châteauneuf-du-Pape, walking past the same farmhouse. The chimney is gone, but the Fabre-Abeille cousins are still there, older, a bit bigger . . . But what's much, much bigger is their wine house, Mont Redon. The great American wine merchant Frank Schoonmaker had discovered the house and launched them in the U.S. The cousins didn't remember me, but we did another tasting, and they were just as generous as the first. That year, I thought I was going to retire from the hotel business, and it seemed to be the closing of a perfect circle. My first private tasting as a hotel man and my last, with wines from the same vineyard."

"Killer," I said.

"What's killer?"

"Me," I said.

"Yes, you're a killer. You sure are. You're my little killer of men." He gave me a thumbs-up.

"It's a killer story, I mean," I clarified.

"Oh, yes. It's nice, *hein*? Anyway, that's it. That's the story. Keep going with the itinerary."

Tired, I rushed through the rest of the names. There were five more houses in Côtes-du-Rhône and another week's worth of visits jammed into two days in the Languedoc region.

I put down the open itinerary and took a break to excavate my belly button for lint and other crusty accumulations.

"This is the wine trip to end all wine trips," he proclaimed.

"Hmm," I said. I said this, but I had begun to think about my ex-boyfriend, Matthew. Gorgeous, shiny-eyed Matthew.

"The most interesting schlep, technically, will be through Languedoc. Big up-and-comer. In the past, just fifteen years ago or so, winemakers didn't understand what kind of lucky climate they had. The wines made in the Languedoc region were *les vins des plâtriers*, as they called them. Wine for stone-workers who'd sit there breathing in dust and crap all day and were glad to drink even the crappiest of wines . . ."

Dense fatigue cloaked my face like a goose-down comforter. I missed Matthew. When we split up, I became consumed with the narcissistic terror of what life would be like without his admiration. As my father went on and on about Languedoc, I wondered if I had it in me. The big *it*. The intelligence, the ability to remember, the palate, the vocabulary, the *talent* for wine. If Matthew were standing in the corner of the room, he would have wrapped his absurdly long arms around me and said, "You are the smartest woman I've ever known." And I would have believed the hyperbole. But in that moment, I felt as though I knew nothing. *I am taking this trip to prove to my father that I am what he already thinks I am, but I am actually not so sure that who he thinks I am is who I really am.* A yawning panic blasted through me. It was the same feeling that would overtake me in the cellar during his monologues. *Maybe this trip will prove that I am not good enough to be this man's daughter. The wine will call my bluff.*

Matthew had written me a letter before I left Toronto to meet my father here. A week after our breakup, as a parting gift, an emotional bribe, or a conciliatory gesture, or a little from columns A, B, and C, I'd asked my mother to mail him my father's Peugeot racing bike he was no longer able to pedal, because of his poor, poor knee. Matthew's letter was one of thanks, for the bike, and one of permanent good-bye, to me. To torture myself, or to not forget him, or to ensure that my eye would not wander while in France (or A, B, and C), I'd tucked the letter into my overstuffed wallet, among an old boarding pass from the beginning of the millennium and a receipt for a Caesar salad and a medium Hawaiian pizza and other such detritus. Matthew was younger than me, and my love for him had mutated from passion to compassion in the time we'd been together. It had gone from loverly to motherly. And this was untenable and could not be untransformed. In his letter, he'd written of his terrible love for me, his terrible, debilitating romantic love, and how his heart pumped lead at the thought of being without me. That's what it had said: "My heart pumps lead at the thought of being without you." I'd thought love letters were for weepy, ridiculous people until I'd received this one—and read it and reread it and rereread it, taking maudlin delight in my chest seizing, or my eyes burning, or my head spinning. Dizzy, abstract feelings I wish I'd had for real, and in the positive sense, when we were together. He'd spoken of how he fell in love with me over and over again, whenever I called him Matty, whenever I broke my electric toothbrush, whenever I touched my bangs. If the time had called for a joke, I'd have run up to him, clutching my gut, and said, "Ooh, Matty, you got me right in the feelings. Right in the *feelings*, man." We'd joked our way through all our psychic intimacy, our respective revelations of the tragedies we'd known. He'd cracked a joke that made me snort after I told him about my most terrible day, about an old man dying. But death, for some reason, is funnier than love. This stuff was not the stuff of jokes.

Reflexively, I removed my hand from my belly button area and smoothed my bangs straight, running it down my forehead and face. I sighed a sad sigh and waved the excavation finger under my nose. It smelled like feelings. Crusty old feelings.

I noticed my father had stopped talking and was staring at me.

"ARE YOU SMELLING YOUR BELLY BUTTON?" he bellowed. But his anger was half-assed. He was only feigning reprimand. I turned my head and looked at him with only my unblinking left eye, like a shark, with the criticism only a half-face-shark-face can achieve. This belly button yelling was coming from a man who decadently plunges his ears with Q-tips, then packs the soiled sticks back into his toiletry kit for reuse.

"I'm sorry, Dad."

After pacing around for a little while, he came back to where I was sitting. I flipped to the Languedoc section of the itinerary.

"Dad. I'm sorry. Continue. I was listening," I urged. I jostled my head back and forth, trying to rattle my brain into the correct position, like a CD that needs to be poked into its place in the tray so it can actually play music.

"Yes. You listen to *me*. When it comes to smelling parts of your body, I know. I have an automatic radar for this stuff. I might miss a lot in life, but not in these areas," he admonished.

"I know, I know. I know. I do," I said. *It is your duty to dispose of this habit before getting off the plane*, I thought. *He has set this whole thing up for you, dammit.*

I made a vow to study the Languedoc section and the rest of the sections later, when I was less tired and more together. As I closed the booklet, I read the last line, which had been written by whomever my father had tasked with the transcription. It said, "Youpi! *Le voyage va être formidable!* Good luck and have a marvelous safari!"

chapter three

After kissing my father on both cheeks and bidding him good night, I shut myself into my bedroom in the Montreal suite. I sat on my bed, nervously folding and refolding my underwear, which sat at the top of my open turquoise backpack. I always pack the underwear on top. *Fifteen hundred kilometers with this man, in a car.* I thought about the geographic and philosophical breadth of the trip. My lip tingled. This meant a cold sore was brewing. I get them when I'm stressed. Typically, they grow so large and puffy, I look like I have a harelip.

He was so excited, telling that old story about Fabre-Abeille, about the circle of wine, of life. Wine as life. *Such a bland metaphor, so trite and easy!* But as channeled through my father, it was the opposite: epic, sweeping, full of pure emotion and genuine faith. During the retelling of the story, he'd even stopped stuffing croutons into his mouth.

I recalled a moment I'd witnessed several years earlier, one Christmas, when I'd been folding paper napkins with pictures of cartoon reindeers on them. My dad had been in his cellar, choosing bottles for our Christmas Day tasting. I'd heard a loud crash and a choked scream. I thumped down the basement stairs, rounding the corner into the wine cellar.

Splayed on the nubbly concrete like some big, disturbed animal was my dad, panting nervously over a big splash of oozing dark red liquid. In his right hand was a spoon, which he was using to scrape along the floor to collect the thinnest layers of the fluid. Every three or four scrapes, he'd insert the tip of the spoon into his mouth and tentatively suck dry the little pool he'd accumulated. He'd stop for a moment to swish the liquid around, then stick out his tongue and tap at it to make sure he wasn't swallowing glass.

"Dad," I'd said.

"Oh, Toots . . ." He gazed up at me with pathetic, watery eyes.

"What happened?"

"I was getting this lovely Port for us." He dropped the spoon and flattened his hand, moving it all around the cellar, indicating the shambled state of the bottle and its contents. "And I *treeped* and fell and the bottle fell and now it is broken and lost forever."

"That's bad news, Dad. Was it an expensive bottle?"

"Yes. Ah, yes. But who cares about expensive? It was a Taylor, Fladgate from 1945."

I stared at him blankly.

"Nineteen forty-five," he repeated.

"The evacuation from Auschwitz?" I'd offered. That was one thing I knew about 1945. My paternal grandfather had been part of an organization that helped move Jewish orphans from France to Switzerland and Spain during the war.

"No. Come on. Come on, Toots—1945. An *extraordinary* year for Port. One of the best of the twentieth century."

"Riiiiiiiight . . . 1945. Of course. A classic year." I had repeated this deliberately, hoping to sound convincing—if not in my fake understanding, then in what had been my real empathy.

I stuffed the little squares of underwear back into my bag. I had packed some lacy things, in case the trip revealed to me a handsome young tryst-worthy vineyard owner. Guilt made my head pound. This trip was not for trysts! I solemnly reached for my satchel and fished around for my wallet, snapped it open, and unfolded Matthew's letter. I read the line I loved and hated the most, out of all the lines that had probably ever been written to me on the subject of love: "If we can't be together, I have to start the long, painful process of falling out of love with you." I puzzled over the idea of one-way chemistry. Matthew had burrowed his way into me, and I was somehow incapable of dropping to my hands and knees and crawling into him. There was too much muck involved, too much faith required. So he was abandoning me, because I was not—or could not become—motivated to love him properly. I felt stupid and cowardly and dry inside.

I tried to think of one relationship—with a human, with

an object, with a concept—where I'd experienced alchemy. Something irrational and magical had happened when I'd met my first love, Peter. But everything exceptional about that love was ruined quickly, because of bad luck and worse timing.

Meanwhile, my father seemed to have an unlimited capacity for it. He waited three patient, silent years to capture my mother. His love of me and my three brothers was at times bafflingly articulated, yes, but generally full of devotion and democratic respect. He had a pious and limitless dedication to history and conjured its ghosts at will. He and Bach went on trips together; his head dropped in sadness as he spoke of champion French boxer Marcel Cerdan's love affair with Edith Piaf. He owned a six-hundred-page book on cat psychology. He'd run eight marathons, clocking his best time of 3:03 when he was fifty-five years old. And the alchemical reaction that occurred when he drank wine was lyrical. It was as though every component of his face and skull—his swishing mouth, his deep and generously fascinated expression, his flared nostrils—were all having a smooth, unspoken dialogue with the liquid in the glass, and the conclusion they'd reached was some great and secret human truth. How could I learn to love like that? How could I show him I shared that capacity? *In two weeks?*

I drew the diaphanous white screens and then the heavy, opaque curtains halfway across the cold cobalt blue of the window so that I would be woken up by the sun, rather than by my father's habit of storming into my dark room in a hotel-issue bathrobe and pinching one of my big toes until I screamed a curse at him. Turning around, I eyed the itinerary that I'd chucked into the middle of the comforter. I swaddled myself in the crispy sheets and picked it up again. There were little wine-themed graphics on each page. Curly vines, jagged leaves, small circles representing grapes. The title of the program was in large red letters: *"SAFARI VINICOLE EN TERRE DE FRANCE: de son Honneur le Maréchal P. Borel et son aide-de-camp."* Our French wine safari: for the honorable Field Marshal Philippe Borel and his camp assistant.

That was me, the nameless camp assistant.

Earlier in the evening, before story time, I'd asked him, "Aide-de-camp? That's my role?"

He'd answered, "That's a high-rank position. You should be wearing a ceremonial golden braid."

"But I don't have a braid. I don't even have a name. I am braidless and nameless."

He'd looked at me silently.

"Dad."

Ignoring me, he'd slowly lifted an empty plastic water bottle off a marble-topped coffee table and then, quick quick, he'd begun shaking it and wiggling his ass to an imaginary cha-cha beat, singing, *"Maracas! Marrrrrrracas!"*

I shook my head at the itinerary. The nameless camp assistant, assisting the most honorable Philippe Borel. The joke amplified my feelings of being small and stupid and without heart. I counted our scheduled visits and winery tours.

Alsace, Burgundy, Côtes-du-Rhône, Languedoc. I flipped the page, expecting to count those in Bordeaux. But there was no other section, only typed-out directions and more accompanying maps. Flipping through the package again, I scanned each page. No Bordeaux. Perfect. In our years of cellar-bound dad/daughter wine lessons and countless tastings, only one nugget of information about wine had stuck readily, easily. I'd use it as a point of pride when reminiscing about my Euro-influenced childhood to strangers I wanted to impress. And for this trip, it was my one saving grace, my one instant access point of reference within what was beginning to seem like an endless landscape of French grapes and zero feelings. My memorized knowledge of Bordeaux was the earliest lesson my father had imposed that had managed to gain any traction.

For the record, it was this.

There are five producers of Grand Cru wines in the Bordeaux region of France. The term *Grand Cru* refers to the highest level of classification in winemaking. If you are drinking a Grand Cru wine, you are drinking the best wine from that winemaking region, in the year that particular Grand Cru was produced. In Bordeaux, there are five winemaking houses that make wine good enough to bestow with the classification of Grand Cru: Château Margaux, Château Mouton-Rothschild, Château Lafite, Château Latour, and Château Haut-Brion.

I pulled the comforter up to my chin and reached up and behind me to turn off the light. On the desk across the room was an old phone, its orange message light blinking inexplicably. I wanted to call Matthew to say a final, final good-bye, but I resisted. Maybe I wanted to tell him to not fall out of love with me just yet, to just love me enough for two until I learned how to unclench my own chemical reaction for him. I did not get up. If we could fix our future, or if something could be tweaked or modified in the name of some kind of sexless but enduring friendship, it could wait two weeks. The world was an elastic-band ball of future. Fourteen days would not cause that ball to disappear.

—◌⌒

In the morning, in the airport, my father and I divided and shared a panini while waiting for our plane to board. The arugula inside was a bit limp, like me. I picked and poked and took small bites, fretting about my cold sore, which had developed overnight into a magnificent blister. My dad chomped through his section of the sandwich with a vengeance that would indicate that it was responsible for the sacking and burning of his ancestral village. Bordeaux was still on my mind.

"Why are we not doing Bordeaux?" I asked in a small voice.

"Fuck Bordeaux!"

"Fuck Bordeaux," I repeated. "Okaaaaay . . ."

"Yes, fuck it."

"Why?"

"Speculators. Wines from Bordeaux are a market, just like any other market . . . stocks, art, anything. Speculators come to Bordeaux and make predictions about the quality of the wine. What kind of year will it be? Is it worth investing? This kind of stuff. The big names from Bordeaux . . ."

"MoutonMargauxLafiteLatourHaut-Brion!" The five châteaux fly out of my mouth, fast and smooth as ball bearings covered in Crisco.

"Very good, Toots. These big names, the Lafites and the Latours, are well known. Like a painting by Chagall or Monet. People know these names of Bordeaux. Châteaux produce a finite number of bottles a year. Once a price is set, immediately ninety percent of these wines will disappear to market makers, who then, if their predictions come true, will turn around and sell them at inflated prices."

"Market makers. Like hype men for hip-hop MCs." I nodded furiously.

"Like who?"

"Never mind. Go on." I made my head go still.

"These people are driving up the prices of Bordeaux. The prices are balloons. I don't buy balloons. I am alert. I am vigilant. I go for the deal. The deal can happen at any time, but it is not happening in Bordeaux. Especially not this year. Two thousand five has a buzz. A *beeg* buzz. There is a *beeg* buzz around this year. It will be extraordinary in all of France. All the magazines say so. *Wine Spectator. Decanter.* They follow the harvest of all the vintners and are saying this is going to be an awesome year. Everything is set up for it to be extraordinary. It's what happened during the previous season. Rain. Lack of rain. Dryness of the soil. A bright October, not too dry. The winter was even. No surprises. Two thousand four laid the foundation for 2005 to be a potentially great season. So FUCK Bordeaux and its speculators, *hein*?" He pressed out a sigh, tight-lipped, as if he were blowing air through a straw. He punctuated the monologue by throwing a meatless bit of focaccia down on the sweaty green tray.

"Yeah. Right. Okay. Fuck them, then!" I agreed. I loved fucking. Them, I mean. Those people, fuck THEM! He was so mad! Rants, I could retain.

The inside of the plane was quiet and dark blue and humming with engine sounds and the startled breathing of its semiasleep passengers. There were five hours to go before we touched down on the tarmac in Paris, and my father had disappeared. We booked our tickets separately, so as we boarded the plane, I lost him in a row around the early twenties, on my way to row 4,291.

This was vaguely worrisome. I fidgeted in my seat, wanting to spider-leg, for the third time, over the body of my slumbering neighbor to search the plane for him. My dad was overcoming a supervirus left over from a recent African safari adventure, but he hadn't experienced any symptoms in the days leading up to our wine safari adventure . . . I was flummoxed.

He had dematerialized.

Perhaps not. Perhaps he was sleeping and had covered his face with a blanket.

Or not. Earlier, I had done a careful audit of each seat, scanning for his royal blue polo shirt with gold stripes. The search had turned up nil.

He was gone!

It was possible he had fallen asleep in a bathroom stall.

With nothing left to do, I turned my head and tried to distinguish hamster shapes in the black clouds hanging in the navy sky outside the plane's window. I wondered what would happen next.

This trip would be a phenomenal success. In history, it would be described the way movie reviewers are quoted on the backs of DVDs: "A touching, poignant tale of a father and a daughter seeking unity in the vineyards of France. Funny, bizarre, full of pathos."

This trip would be a spectacular failure. We would never speak again.

I remembered how disappointed he'd become during the Christmas tasting—that same day I'd found him drinking his 1945 Taylor, Fladgate off the floor. We'd been sitting around the table in the middle of the afternoon, tasting a 1961 Clos des Mouches. I was sipping faster than my father, mother, and my younger brother, Nico, and was tipsy enough to dare to make an analysis. The rest of the family had been peering into their glasses, saying nothing. Waving my glass around in a fit of similes and desire to connect, I'd hazarded:

"This seems fledgling, full of potential, but was too young to be drunk. It's like the wine is a proud little boy at an adult cocktail party in a sharp tuxedo and hair he's slicked with such diligence that it crackles when touched, looking up at the adults, knowing that—not now, not even ten years from now, but someday—he will be the life of a party like this one. But not now, not yet." I leaned back and closed my eyes for effect. When I opened them, my father was driving his fingertips into his temples, his two eyebrows smashed into one angry caterpillar.

"The wine is corked, Tou Tou," he'd said.

I looked down at my third glass of cheap white wine that sat in the circular indentation of my tray table. I chugged it in two gulps and opened my mouth slightly, drawing in air to let the musty, unpleasant flavors develop. *Armpits of woolen coat, socks, that weird bush I once smelled by a bog in Florida.* Dejectedly, I flopped my head back into my seat cushion and bounced it a few times. Maybe I was too lazy or dumb. I despised almost all poetry. I'd developed a Coca-Cola habit in university that would cripple me with gut rot. Grilled cheese sandwiches swimming in ketchup. Ripped flannel shirts and days-old underwear. Cracked IKEA cereal bowls I refused to throw out. Electric fireplaces. Puffy toilet seats.

Shuddering with premature embarrassment over what I saw as the inevitability of failure at the tastings over these coming days, I squeezed my eyes shut and forced myself to be lulled into a headachy sleep of bad wine and cold, synthetic plane air.

I woke up to another bumping food cart and ate my eastern standard time night breakfast, meaning my Greenwich mean time breakfast breakfast. Dry little croissants and orange juice made from oranges that are made of other biochemical elements. Dust, sodium sulfate, hippo tallow, agar. Science-experiment orange juice. I shamefully relished every bit of the badness, and in my gluttonous haste I'd even swallowed a piece of the red wax that sheathed the Babybel cheese. Perking up a bit from the injection of sugar, I thought of my father, temporarily forgetting he'd gone missing. *The point of this trip is to learn from his guidance. Fifteen hundred kilometers in a car with that man! He is my sherpa, and I am receptive. I am alert! Proximity and willingness can give way to chemistry. I just have to relax!*

The cabin lights went off, the plane landed and sneezed to a stop. I rose and collected my things. I peeked over passenger heads, being careful not to jostle them with my carry-on luggage and pieces of my dad's carry-on luggage, which he had gallantly bequeathed to me before I walked the aisle mile to my seat. No peppery head appeared in the distance. I lumbered toward the exit.

Where was this man?

The pale French morning sun blundered through the airport windows. In spite of my fatigue from the fretting and the jet lag, I was overcome with the prickly excitement one gets from being in another country with its different smells, foreign McDonald's menus, and drugstore products that somehow seem more effective than the ones at home. I bobbed and weaved. Still no Philippe.

Then, at the luggage turnstile, one Philippe Borel appeared. One Philippe Borel with one clayey face and one frowny mouth, shiny with saliva.

"PAPA!" I called. His head whipped up and his eyes crossed briefly. One hand attempted a wave, then dropped down as slowly as it went up.

Approaching his hunched figure, I made my palm into a cup, then placed it lightly on his stubbly cheek.

"I am very sick," he said breathily.

"You look very sick." I paused. Bad news was imminent. "Why are you very sick?"

"Plane food," he said.

"Plane food," I repeated. "Plane food, plane food," I repeated and repeated. This was a 1990s stand-up comedy routine. How about that plane food! (Canned laughter.)

"Bad chicken. Bad something. I don't know, Tootsie."

"So that's where you were during the flight." Now I understood.

"In the bathroom," he replied.

"Right."

"Vomiting. So much," he said.

"Right. All right." An inauspicious beginning.

Bags came off the turnstile, rental car keys found their way into his hand.

I heaved all the bags into the trunk of the hatchback Citroën Picasso he'd rented. I shuffled tentatively from left to right, not knowing whether I was required in the driver's seat. Before I could do anything decisive, he slumped behind the wheel, though it was clear he should not be driving. This was easy to see—he had just accidentally backed into one of the concrete walls in the airport's underground parking lot.

"Are you sure you don't want me to drive?" I offered.

"No, Tootsen. Thank you. I am fine. You navigate."

Before we left the parking lot, I forced him to drink a liter of Perrier. He steadied his hands on the wheel, belched loudly, and we were off, along the French highway, small European cars zipping by us on all sides. He was becoming steadier with every kilometer. Great. Good. What was left of my limp-arugula anxiety faded into post-airplane orange juice stokedness. *We will laugh! We will tell each other secrets! We will invent a new language, for ourselves and for wine! This is significant!*

I wanted to share a laugh with him, the inaugural laugh of the trip, the laugh that would set it all off. Traffic had seized up around us a bit, so I leaned into the front panel of the Picasso and pressed my index finger into the area below the hazard light button. I looked at my dad, who was looking at me, and drummed my finger on the spot over and over while screeching, "Beee-ooo! . . . Beee-ooo, bee-bee-bee-OOO!"

"What are you doing?" he asked.

"I'm vaporizing the traffic with the car's laser," I said.

"What laser?"

"The *laser*, you know."

He got it. He cheered up. "Where did you learn to do this?"

"It's something Matthew and I do when we want people to get out of our way. Or die," I responded.

He cackled and brushed my hand away, replacing it with

his own. He made a French accent laser sound. "Pyoo . . . Pyoo, pyoo PYOO!"

We both bee-ooo'ed and pyoo'ed our heads off until we were laughing like insane people. The traffic eventually vaporized and we turned off the highway onto a smaller road, driving through perfect little French villages built of brown and gray stones, flowerpots overflowing with Lego-like petals of yellow and orangey red and hot pink, everything dusty and bright in the white early afternoon sun.

We stopped for lunch in one of the villages close to the city of Troyes, about halfway between Paris and Contrexéville. My father, who had receded back into nausea and frailty, attempted to straighten the car between two other cars and was using the age-old art of Braille parking—slamming our car into the bumper of the car in front, then the bumper of the car behind, until it was nestled comfortably between them and next to the curb. We walked to the village *boulangerie*. I chose a ham sandwich, the best sandwich you could get in this country, this country of transcendent ham sandwiches where the meat is slow-roasted and generously stacked in perfect pink strips between a bumpy layer of cold fresh butter and a baguette that is crusty and dark blond outside, soft, fragrant, and yeasty inside. We located the cobbled town square, which was deserted. Sitting on the steps of the church, I waved my sandwich in front of my father's face. He could only stomach plain bread and was sadly tearing off little pieces, rolling the squishy dough between his fingers before pushing them into his mouth.

"You look like you're about to pass out. Really, Dad, I'll drive the rest of the way. You can navigate," I offered again, this time punching my words more, as though I'd acquired a medical degree in the last two hours and me driving meant the difference between life and death.

"Okay, Tootsen. Aye-aye. Fine, then. You are the captain."

Minutes into my reign as the captain, we became lost. I was experiencing a mental block when it came to understanding the subtleties in the arrow directions in French roundabouts and ended up bailing onto a road too early. We found ourselves in a town that looked like all the other towns we'd passed. I slowed the car when I saw an ancient woman sitting outside her house on a rickety stool. My father poked his head out of the window.

"*Pardonnez-moi, madame. On cherche la route pour Contréxeville.*" (Excuse me, ma'am, we're looking for the road to Contréxeville.)

She nodded, and the two mumbled to each other for a few minutes. My father thanked her with an excessive amount of gusto, as though she'd just given him directions to Eldorado.

"*Merci, madame, merci merci, merci infiniment, oui, oui, merci, merci infiniment.*"

He turned and stared out the windshield. "Did you get that?" he asked.

"Get what?"

"What the old broad said."

"Uh, no. That's your job as navigator. You didn't listen to her directions?"

"No, I thought you were listening."

"No."

"Oh."

I silently fumed over what I saw as selfishness—I was tired too, after all—but I contained myself and pressed evenly on the accelerator.

We came to another roundabout and noticed a trucker who had pulled over.

"I'll ask this guy, maybe, huh, Dad? He'll probably know where Contrexéville is." I was careful not to weight my voice with any anger or exhaustion.

The trucker gave new directions, so I drove. My dad was sleeping when we arrived at the hotel—a repurposed castle called the Cosmos. I shook him awake, I hauled the bags without his help, we checked in. We ordered room service, the waiter knocked too violently and delivered chicken that was undercooked in the middle. The smell of it sent Dad running into the bathroom for another fit of autodecontamination. When he emerged we spent a few hours in silence, reading drowsily and waiting for the evening to bring us an hour that would be appropriate enough to fall asleep and trick our bodies into adjusting to the new time zone.

Later, when the sky was mostly dark and we were tucked into our tiny single beds, my father was lying awake, looking at the ceiling with a small, satisfied smile on his face.

"You're smiling. Are you feeling better?" I asked.

He shook his head like one of those spring-necked dogs taxi drivers keep on their dashboards. "No. I am thinking about the waiter. That fucking waiter. To knock like that. Bullshit. Unprofessional. And the chicken. Disgusting. I am smiling because I am looking forward to giving the front desk staff some shit tomorrow for all this."

"Oh," I said, immediately suppressing my panic. I wanted sleep. I wanted the new day to begin, and I wanted the chance to prove wrong my fears about the trip. I lay there, trying to twist his cruelty into something good. *If he's well enough to humiliate us tomorrow morning, it's possible he'll be well enough to prevent me from humiliating myself during my first real tasting.*

I wanted to tell him this thought.

"Dad?"

But he had already begun to snore.

chapter four

A detour.

Two days after my father's sixty-second birthday, I killed an old man with my car.

If the weather of 2004 had arranged for 2005 to be buzzed about as a classic vintage in France, it was that big occurrence that created the conditions for our wine trip. It began with a car accident and a joke. On February 23, 2001, I hit the old man. Three days later, my father made a joke about it.

He made the joke as we were driving to the Quebec City airport. My university reading week was over. We were cruising along the same road upon which I had killed the old man.

At two p.m., I would board a plane back to Halifax, where I would sob and nap my way through my last semester with a head that felt as though it were full of seawater. Three months later, a little thinner and much older, I would numbly accept the degree for my honors Bachelor of Journalism. A few days after that, I would study the calligraphy on the degree and see that I had received an honors BJ. I laughed hard at my honors BJ, but not as hard as I laughed at my father's joke.

My father wanted to drive me to the airport, even though he has never been the to-the-airport-driving type of father, and my mother has always been the quintessential to-the-airport-driving type of mother. He had said all the wrong things after the police called the house and reported to my teenage brother, Nico, that the old man had died in the hospital from head trauma. When the call came in and Nico relayed the news of the death, my father picked up the phone and spoke with the police officer who was handling the paperwork. An hour or so later, I arrived home from the gym, where I'd spent an hour running on the treadmill, looking at my eyes and the bags underneath them in the mirrors that lined the walls. He got up from the sofa, fumbling a bit as he pushed himself into a standing position. He stood too far away from me and began to talk. His voice was clumsy and unsure. He said, "I thought you might like to know a little bit more about the man who you *keeled*." He paused and his eyes flickered around, absorbing my reaction. He was searching, I think, for either a softening or a hardening. There was a hollow feeling in the back of my face. *Dead. It happened. I made it happen. I created a death.* I thought of the cracking thud his body had made as it connected with the metal of the car. The blood. Unsurprised, I stood still in front of my father.

Two thoughts crawled around in there like beetles. I wanted to know about him. I wanted to know all about him. Knowing might be some kind of punishment. A proper repercussion. But also, it had been an accident. I was a killer, not a murderer. I was just an accidental killer. *A killer!* I thought, amazed. I nodded at my father to keep going.

"He was eighty-three, and a pharmacist. He was from France. I want to tell you his name, maybe it will help you, to know some more about him. His name was . . ." *That's enough for the killer.* I held up my hand and stopped him, and ran with small shuffling steps to my room, my spine as stiff as a crowbar, my face spewing the kinds of tears you see only in cartoons. Anime tears. The ones that spring from your eyes horizontally instead of vertically. I shut the door and stared at my face again, watching how the tears made my eyes as bright as leaves. I waited. *He should be coming in now. He will be coming in any minute now to acknowledge that we both didn't know what we were doing back there, sharing details about something that does not yet make any sense.* My tears dried up. I walked over to the edge of the bed and sat down, breathing so that my ribs were as big and open as they could be. I watched my ribs move in and out for a long time. Too many minutes passed. Eventually, he knocked and poked his head in, his face pointed toward the carpet. "Are you ready for dinner? I have made you some fish," he offered. I didn't like fish back then.

The road to the airport was slippery with little fresh flakes that looked more like sand than snow. The car smelled faintly of his pipe tobacco and the body lotion my father would steal from his hotel's housekeeping carts to rub into the leather upholstery with an old, gross hand towel, also stolen from the hotel. When he did this, he would drop his voice to a baritone, like that of a wealthy, new-money creep who vacations in Monte Carlo, and say, "Apply liberally. Apply LIBERALLY! Heheheheh!!" Sitting on these shiny and slightly greasy seats, we drove in silence down the speckled road where three days earlier I hit the man and watched him ricochet sideways off the hood of my mom's kelly green GMC Jimmy. The man was jaywalking with his breakfast groceries, all of which shot up into the sky like a food geyser and landed around him in an eerie circle just one second later. When I screeched the truck to a stop and barreled out of it, I saw that some of his groceries were spattered with blood: the economy-size box of Special K and a bag of puffed rice. As I watched some more blood leak from his wrinkly ear and form a pool, I thought, *He sure does like cereal.* Special K was my university nickname from freshman year. I thought about how I'd have to tell my friends back in Halifax to refrain from using my nickname. For many interminable, sickening moments, I absorbed his image; I sucked him up like ink in a quill: his frail white body as crumpled as a puppet cut from its strings, his outfit of navy blue Wellingtons, navy blue ski hat and down-filled coat, navy blue mittens and nylon pants, an inch or two of navy blue thermal underwear peeking out from where his pant leg had scrunched up. Then I wailed and wailed and covered my face with my cold hands and screamed, "I'm so sorry!" The breathy heat from the words blew back into my face. I screamed some more. Some people had started to form a circle around the old man, others were on their cell phones, calling ambulances. I thought of a lifesaving course I'd taken a thousand years ago. RED. The acronym for bleeding wounds. Rest, elevate, direct pressure. *Unless the neck is broken. If the neck might be broken, wait for the ambulance.* A curly-haired woman was kneeling close to the old man's feet. I lunged at her and swatted her hands away from his body. "Please, give him space. He needs space to breathe." I said those words hoarsely, not sure if I'd rendered him incapable of breathing. My boyfriend Peter, who had been sitting in the passenger seat, ran toward me with my woolen winter coat. Through my blurry eyes, he was a big manta ray man, running like that with my long gray coat outstretched. Even though I'm more afraid of manta rays than any other creature, I shoved my face into Peter's turtleneck and gripped his waist as he folded himself and the coat around my quaking body and said, "Borel. This was not your fault." Right before the ambulance arrived, the old man stirred and opened his eyes. I grabbed the lapel of Peter's coat and scrunched it hard, hoping.

My father sped up along the road, as he is French and has the French stupid-fast-driver gene. Not far in the distance, we saw a shape step off the sidewalk. It was an old man. Not as old as the one I killed, but quite old nonetheless. My hand was twitching—just about to rise up and slap my own forehead and face to cover my eyes—when my father made the joke. He pressed his foot onto the gas, turned to me with quizzical eyebrows, and said, "What do you think, should we make it two for two?"

It hurt to laugh at this, but I hadn't forgotten how to laugh. I don't believe those tragic people when they look at you with their condescending puppy-puddle eyes and say, "I've forgotten how to laugh." Like hell you've forgotten, you illogical tragic puppy-puddle-eyed self-important asshole! So I laughed just like I knew how, but my throat hurt when the sound pushed out.

"Thanks for making that joke, Dad."

He nodded and continued to step on the accelerator. The old man scurried across the lane and made it safely to the sidewalk. My father cackled. His cackle is twisted and intense, as though he's accidentally swallowed feathers from a sparrow's chin and is attempting to force them out his trachea. If one were to record his laugh and download it into a supercomputer that deconstructs the emotional significance of vocal tones, the laser printout of the analysis (sectioned into a nice, color-coded pie graph) would look something this:

Mirth (Light Blue) = 29%
Cruelty (Puce) = 12%
Affectation (Goldenrod) = 15%
Delight in the expression of detachment/
    unconventionality (Forest Green) = 41%
Madness (Periwinkle Blue) = 3%

I laughed and he cackled until he pulled up to the departures entrance of Quebec's then squat and grimy airport. Snow fell on the windshield and melted, tiny stars turned to blobby droplets. I listened to the hydraulic explosions of planes taking off, waiting for him to drive into the parking lot so that we could have a proper airport good-bye, near the security gate, where dads are meant to say good-bye to their daughters after their daughters have just undergone the age-old ritual of killing old men with their cars.

"Okay, Tou Tou," he said with finality.

It seemed this proper airport good-bye was not in the cards.

"Ehm. Right. Can you pop the trunk?"

The trunk went *vvvjjeeeet.*

We embraced awkwardly in the cold. He couldn't get his arms around my body and my turquoise backpack, which slumped over my back and shoulders. Instead, he held the side straps of the bag and pulled me into something that resembled a half-assed calisthenics exercise. My forehead pressed into his Adam's apple. His sweater smelled of pipe and something minty. I wished he were parking the car, walking me into the airport, standing with me in line to get my boarding pass. Buying me a muffin. Treating me to some magazines for the flight. Waving at me one last time from the security threshold.

"Thanks for driving me," I said.

"Thanks for coming," he answered.

"I love you," I said.

"I love you so much," he answered. "*Zees* next months will be hell for you. It will be very hard for you to digest," he added.

My eyes stung. I nodded and turned on my heels, slipping a bit, dazed by his capacity to say the truth at exactly all the wrong moments.

For a long time after the accident, I felt that stupid jay-walking old man and I ruined each other's life. He was dead, real dead for sure; but God, that was the easy part, to be so goddamned dead. For Christ's sake, that was an easy ruin-ation. Concerning my own ruination, at first, in moments, I did not see it that way at all. It was not ruination, but the sad-dest glory. During my first days back on campus, as the news of the killing spread and morphed and eventually turned into gossip, I was glad. Proud, occasionally. I heard that a boy named Dave had whispered, "Does she need a lawyer?" I imagined others asking, "She hasn't been in class, is she on lithium and heroin and Southern Comfort and going in-sane?" I loved this. I loved it when I wasn't in my bedroom, fully clothed and surrounded by pillows, contemplating the rest of this life that was unfurling in front of me: a scroll, the first lengths written in careful script, then a big black line, and everything after the line scratched and psychotic and il-legible. I was a twenty-one-year-old with some definition, with an edge like new dental instruments. I was a killing machine, a velociraptor, a badass. If I wanted to become a gangster rap MC or that silent tattooed guy with the socio-pathic glint in his eye who drives the forklift at the mattress warehouse, I probably could just go and do those things, no problem. It excited me in moments, filled me with heat. And then left me freezing. Young people taunt the outside world to bestow upon them meaning, like teenagers who decide to become Wiccans or punks. The old man had done that for me in mere seconds, and it hadn't even required me to burn sage or put Elmer's Glue-All in my hair. My professors didn't say a word when I skipped weeks' worth of classes. And my two roommates never complained when they'd come home and find me supine on the couch, mumbling my way through a hamburger made with one's frozen meat patties that I'd lined with the other's barbecue-flavored potato chips because they'd had the gall to let us run out of actual barbecue sauce.

I had killed, therefore I was untouchable. I flopped around lazily in the womb of my depression. I had limitless prerogative. On some days, it was my dream come true. On others, I became immobile with terror as I considered the litter of slippery baby demons the accident had birthed.

The demons overtook the dream that summer. It happened while I was cooking orzo at my parents' house in Quebec City, in the kitchen where I'd been told the news of the old man and his quiet hospital death.

Nico was going for a bike ride on the Plains of Abraham, where in the eighteenth century the French and the British used to stab at each other with bayonets. He waved to me as he was exiting the big sliding glass door that separated the living room from the world.

"Bye, Tou Tou." His way of pronouncing my nickname was cute: "*Tuh*-too." His floppy blond head bounced out of sight.

"Don't be long! I'm making *ORZO*!!!" I yelled after him, as though the shape of the pasta would determine the length of his ride. My parents had spent the weekend at our home in the woods outside Quebec City. My father had nicknamed it the Camp, as if we were a family of monarchical pedigree. Or a cult, like the Mansons. My father wanted silence and a place to fish.

In the kitchen, I moved from fridge to stove to cabinets as if I were a robot. I accompanied the robot movements with a running internal monologue, done in the voice of a robot. *OP-EN FRIDGE DRAW-ER. TAKE. THE. DILL.* Finding this strange—I'm more of a mad stomper and a flailer—I curved my neck around and wiggled my shoulders to loosen them up. My heart felt as if it were charley-horsed. Funny. I laughed a big laugh at myself, to see if the sonic waves I was creating from my diaphragm and larynx would have a normalizing effect on the organ that lived between them.

There was a medicine ball on my chest. A big, heavy, invisible medicine ball plunked onto my chest by an imaginary personal trainer. Funny feeling.

Nico was going to die on his bicycle ride. I was going to cook this orzo and he'd be too dead to eat it. No. I wouldn't even get to the point of boiling the water for the orzo. My parents would come walking through the glass door and I'd explain that Nico had been in an accident and we had to drive to the hospital immediately. Had Nico ever indicated whether he'd want to be cremated or buried? Our family believed in cremations, generally. But he was only sixteen! Kids who are sixteen have not yet made these decisions. Poor Nico, sideswiped by a pool-cleaning truck. His jaw hanging unhinged, his eyes wide open, frozen in a look of the most unwelcome of all surprises.

I breathed in acutely and focused more robotically than ever on the *mise en place* for the meal. My parents had called me hours before, wondering if I'd mind cooking dinner for the family. They'd be tired after the two-hour drive. "Lovey, we spent the afternoon varnishing the deck. Do you mind fixing something? We love your food," my mother said over the phone in her moderate, lilting British accent. The deck was large; it zagged right around the entire structure. It was important I cook this meal for them.

Meticulously, I shelled and deveined the shrimp, making sure there weren't any errant bits of disgusting shrimp legs in the bowl. I turned the blushing hothouse tomatoes into a smooth *concassé*. I pulled out pots and pans. *YOU. ARE. TAKING. ONE. PAN. FROM. THE. OVEN. DRAW-ER.* I diced shallots, crushed garlic to a paste using salt and the blade of my knife. I put those in a little bowl. A half lemon sat next to a small strainer I would use to catch the seeds. Butter, oil, placed in a two-item row next to the stovetop. Fresh dill weed, cut from its stalk.

I went round and round the kitchen, placing these bowls in order, adjusting the pan and pot handles so they were not hanging carelessly off the front of the stove. My muscles were that of a startled cat. When would they come home? Were they home yet? I bumped into an open drawer and backed into the stove, causing the large pot of water for the orzo to splash. "Fuck," I exclaimed. "Fuck. Fuck." They weren't going to make it home. There would be terrible smashings and crunchings of metal and bone. One of them would fly through the windshield. The other would die right away from shock and a broken heart. Ambulances would arrive, but it would be too late. Cars and emergency vehicles and startled passersby on mobile phones would form a blinking circle around the corpse and the glass shards and the pools of blood.

I stood very still and tried to focus on the strategy of the meal. First, heat the pan. Then, add the oil until it shines and the butter until it foams. Drop in the shallots, let them sweat. Next, the garlic. Be careful not to burn it, or it will become bitter and chewy and ruin the meal. Deglaze with white wine.

Checking in the fridge for wine, I found a half bottle of Oyster Bay Sauvignon Blanc lying on its side, next to the milk. Good. *THERE. IS. WINE. THIS. WINE. IS. FROM. NEW. ZEALAND.*

Deglaze with white wine. Add the tomatoes. Squeeze the lemon into the pan. Stir together. Season with salt and pepper.

What was the point of this? They would all be dead. I was cooking dinner for a family of ghosts.

Perfect, I thought. This was, in fact, perfect. *If they are all dead, no one will care if I kill myself, then.* Wait. *Peter might care.* I stopped thinking of suitable methods of suicide, for the sake of my loving boyfriend, who loved me dearly. He'd lost his father in a car accident the year before he rode shotgun for mine. I felt guiltier about this than anything else. Anything else in life.

I will fill my vein with a large dose of heroin. I am not steely enough to slit my wrists or jump off a building. Maybe vodka and many, many lorazepams. I nodded silently to myself.

Peter would definitely care. *But he'll get over it,* I told myself. There would be a mass funeral for all the Borels, and that would be our sad story. My father was an important player in the city, a quasi celebrity, really. We'd probably make the front page of a few of the province's French newspapers, at least. Peter could report on it, because he was a CBC reporter. That'd be nice. Fitting. Reverent, in a civic sort of way: "The Borels are all dead. The end. *Fin.* Peter Armstrong, signing off for CBC news in Quebec City."

Nico came home first, sweating and misted with park dust.

"Hey, Toots," he yelled, bumping his bike over the track of the sliding door and scooting it into the front hallway. He turned the corner into the bathroom, and I heard the lock go *click.*

Everyone told me to drive. In my last month at school, my radio skills professor implored me to see her shrink. She had been through a divorce, and he had "really saved my life."

When I sat down across from his potted fern and question-
ably patterned sweater, he said, "One thing is for sure. You
feel bad. You feel bad for long periods of time, then you don't
feel bad for a short period of time. Little by little, those periods of time when you feel bad will start to contract, and the
time between them when you feel okay will begin to expand.
And then one day, the bad periods will disappear altogether."
He paused and then asked, "You're still driving, right? You
should drive." I told him I had driven to my mom's embroi-
dery studio right after I had completed the police report at
the site of the accident. She and Peter and I had gone to a
coffee shop and talked about the scene, the blood, the man,
my head. She made small sympathetic noises and covered my
hand with her hand and gave me lots of squeezes, like little
heartbeats. She asked if I was stable enough to drive back to
the house. I said yes. I said, "Yes, YES!" to all these concerned
citizens who didn't know what to ask and so they asked of
my driving skills (terrific!), of where I wanted to drive (everywhere!), of how much I loved driving (so much!), of why
driving was important (oh, you know!).

"Good!" the shrink said. "Keep it up."

I was not afraid of handling a car. My driving skills had
become tack sharp. Since February, I had undergone a meta-
morphosis. Behind the wheel, I was like one of those insects
with compound eyes that could see everything at once, no
matter how fast it was coming. A dragonfly or a bee. An
all-seeing insect who could even perceive the polarization
of light.

I pictured my parents' old human eyes, dopey and heavy-lidded, weightily drooping with fatigue and glazed with varnish fumes. Maybe no one would even be around to see the accident. One of them would misjudge a turn in the road—one of the smaller, less traveled roads—and sail off the side of it. The car would land upside down on the side of a blossoming potato field, crushing them both like a stick of gum at the bottom of an old lady's purse.

I made the sauce with assiduous attention to the heat of the pan, the smell of the ingredients, the timing of the solid and liquid additions. After tasting it, I added a bit of dried thyme and two large pinches of sugar to remove some of the bitterness from the tomatoes.

Finally, there was a clattering outside. I cocked my head down to peer below the cupboards and through the galley area of the kitchen. They were home. They made it. They were alive and home and they had made it.

"Hi, Toots," my dad said.

"Hi, my love," my mom said.

"Hi," I croaked, my body limp as wet tissue paper.

"We have fresh trout for dinner!" my dad announced cavalierly. My mom dropped a load of things she was carrying and went back to the car to pick up another load of things.

"You have what for dinner?" I whispered.

"Trout," he said, lifting up a red-and-white Coleman cooler.

"YOU HAVE WHAT FOR DINNER?" I screamed. I glared at him, then back at the sauce, as though the sauce

61

were in on this sick gag. I began to sob. I flung cuss words at him. He came toward me and I beat his chest with open palms, eventually slouching into his alarmed embrace.

"But you asked me to fix dinner," I cried weakly. It was obvious that nothing could be fixed.

My menu was out the window.

The end.

I had killed someone's father.

The end.

The end the end.

Clamping his hands on my shoulders, he unglued me from his shirt. He looked at me hard, concerned. His voice was grave.

"Tou Tou. Please remember. Your life is no longer your own once you are loved."

I put the sauce in a Tupperware container for another night. He fried the trout, and it was surprisingly delicious.

Eventually, it all became less important. The old man, the orzo, my pain, all of it. Until my dad, in a way, became the butt of his own joke, when I saw that he too would die. One day.

chapter five

"This is not good." My father's brown eyes, heavy-lidded, stared down at his hands with an expression that said, *Oh, hands. I have hands.* His jaw hung open. Salvador Dalí had painted him in the same manner as his droopy watches. The night, for him, had been sleepless and explosive. "It's eleven already? This is not good." My father never slept in.

I inspected him hard with my one open eye. Only one eye opened. The other was puffed shut. We forgot to shut the window before falling asleep and had allowed a swarm of robust northern French mosquitoes to enter and do their wicked bidding. As the jet lag delivered its last blow to the back of my skull like a cast-iron frying pan, I'd heard their kamikaze swoops around my ears. In a silent prayer to the insect gods, I'd whispered, "Anywhere but the cold sore, you guys." They'd obeyed and indulged me by stinging the shit out of my eyelid.

"It'll get better, Dad!" I cheered. My voice was that of a pubescent boy, crackling with uncertainty. On this morning, our little boat was one wave short of a shipwreck. Plus I can't swim very well. I really can't. I had trained for a triathlon once and gave myself two black eyes and a concussion after affixing my goggles too tightly to my face and slamming into the pool wall.

"Toots, if this continues, we'll have to cancel."

"Tomorrow's tastings? That's not a huge deal, Dad. Don't worry."

"No. *Everytheeng.*"

"The trip?"

"Mm-hmm."

"Oh, come on." I tossed aside his comment, but bile sizzled somewhere in me. Yes. I knew he was prone to melodrama. In any other circumstance, on any other trip, I would have humored him. In this context, however, it felt flippant and disrespectful. *Does he even know why I wanted to come here with him? Share this with him? He's not going to die now—he has plane food poisoning. He is going to die later, of death, of REAL DEATH! Has he not read into the symbolism of his damn cellar being his damn story and if I don't feel what he feels about what's in his damn cellar I'll never feel his damn story?* I allowed myself to wallow for a moment in the tacit betrayal that was his utter inability to understand what seemed, to me, at least, like *very simple metaphorical links.*

He'd seen my face turn shadowy and glum.

"I'm sorry—"

"For what? Oh, don't be sorry. We'll get you better." *Good. Okay. He's responding.* I began clawing manically through my satchel to locate the Spasfon brand nausea medicine we bought at the airport. I wanted to dump it all out, grind it up on the mirror, roll up a fifty-euro bill, attach it to his nose, and slam his face down on the glassy desk while scream-ing, "Hoover that shit, DAD! HOOVER IT!" To cancel the trip would be nonsensical. It would prove that God exists, and He is a cruel and vengeful God who loathes daughters and indulges men with abdomen-area problems. It would prove that He has an egregious inability to prioritize tasks and a sense of humor reminiscent of Dante's Inferno. I don't believe in Him, but I would nevertheless write a strongly worded letter. A letter with the strongest words I know. A complaint letter to His ombudsman, including all the much more pressing chores He should be undertaking, such as:

1. Fix Africa.
2. Fix the Middle East.
3. Give us teleportation already!
4. Pick up dry cleaning.

Once He has completed these tasks, *then* He can ironi-cally punish me for ignoring my father while he was trying to share with me pieces of his history through wine. Only then.

"I'm not saying we must cancel the trip. I just want you to get used to the idea. Consider *eet* as an option," my father said woefully.

He'd gone back to being the emperor of defeatism.

"Don't you *start again*."

"Start what again?" he asked, full of innocence.

"Thaaaaat's the game! Thaaaat's the gaaaaame!" I raised my voice, taunting him to remember what kind of spectator he was at my tennis matches, when I'd first started playing competitively.

When we lived in Dallas, my father's job was based out of the Loews Anatole—a behemoth of a hotel with one thousand rooms and three pools and four restaurants and a koi pond and hissing peacocks that roamed the elaborately manicured grounds—and my parents put me in private tennis lessons. The hotel was on a freeway, so we had no neighbors. The only children who were immediately accessible were those who were staying in the hotel with their parents, and they would always leave me after a few days. The tennis lessons helped with the sort of surreal solitary confinement. I'd been playing since I was small, and the pro at the health club said he saw potential in me. By the time we moved to France, I was competing in regional tournaments against girls three and four years older than me. My father would come to the games, not to cheer me on, but to act as a grim commentator when I was losing. He was famous for his prescience, especially when I was down four games in the second set thanks to being matched against hulking girl-women whose serves might as well have been fired from rocket launchers. "That's the game!" he'd say with a long, watery emphasis on the first syllable. "Thaaaat's the game!"

All at once angry with me, or maybe just ashamed, he marched over to the bathroom and locked himself in it. He might not have been admitting it in words, but the horrid sounds that emanated said, *Thaaaat's the game.*

That's not the game, you melodramatic senior citizen. Not on my watch.

A few minutes later, my pallid Jesus-on-the-cross emerged. He looked calmer. I recalibrated.

"Let's go get some food into you, mmmkay?" I would baby him. When my father becomes ill, he must be babied. He finds it helpful to have a little antique bell around so that he can summon members of the family without having to use his voice. A little bell!

As a gesture of solidarity and care, I joined him in a Spartan breakfast of plain toast and bottles of Contrexéville's famed mineral water. We were sitting in a corner of the Cosmos's bright, 1920s-style communal breakfast area, surrounded by sleek businesspeople and suave older travelers leafing calmly through *Le Monde*, fitting their lips around their glazed and creamy and fruity and meaty breakfasts. We did not look like these people; we were dressed functionally, for driving. I felt deeply unattractive with my cold sore and fat eye, while my dad slouched and sighed through his audible cramps. He worked his way into a piece of baguette, chewing meekly, tentatively, like a child who's forced to eat food that is obviously wholesome, like beets or anything not made entirely of sugar. A constellation of rogue crumbs had adhered themselves to his clammy, glistening cheek. He didn't notice, as he was staring openly at a man with a regrettably large Gorbachevesque birthmark on his bald head. I reached over the table and wiped the crumbs off Dadbaby's face with a kindly slapping gesture and resumed my mission to nibble the flat sliced middle of my own baguette into the shape of France. It was easy to do: just five clean diagonal bites around the square of bread, and voilà, buttered France. I inspected it for topographical accuracy and showed it to my father.

"Look, Dad, it's France," I said.

"Very good, Tootsen." He sighed again. His eyes were on me, then down at his own dry bread, then at my little buttered toast-France, which I was about to nibble down to an even smaller France. I am an engaged eater, he knows this. He knows I have always placed a high value on the last bite of food. Carrots, I eat backward, beginning with the fat end that's close to the root, so that I can save the sweet tip for last. I will spend a half hour on a slice of cake, making sure the final tiny portion has the most delectable sponge-to-icing ratio.

My father continued to stare at toast-France.

"Mrrrrughhhh." Groaning through the motion, he lunged his face toward my outstretched hand, grabbed the pentagonal piece in his teeth, and swallowed it. France was lost.

I slammed my fist down, causing the ice in our water glasses to jangle.

"Not cool, Dad," I said.

I only had theories about what motivated his erratic habit of blind, unfeeling entitlement. Perhaps it was because he was a child of the war. And his father, because of his involvement with the Jewish organization, forced the family to move down the length of France, living in squalor and fear of being arrested by the Gestapo. Because he didn't have nice things for such a long time, like little tin cars and fresh oranges. Maybe it was because his father fell ill with emphysema after the family had moved to Canada for a brand-new start, and my father, at thirteen, was obliged to support his parents and baby sister by working as a dish pig in a restaurant. Or because he suffered the psychic repercussions of his impulsive decisions, like getting married too early, at nineteen, to his first wife, who had a temper and threw his first humidor against their apartment wall, causing it to shatter and cigars to fly everywhere. Perhaps it was because he watched my two older half brothers slowly disengage from him and maybe blame him, indirectly, for causing their mother such pain that she eventually died of cancer. I hadn't asked. Maybe it was all of the above, maybe it was none of it. Maybe children don't ask these questions of their parents. Whatever it was, I didn't believe it allowed him to eat the last bite of my toast without asking. As it didn't allow him to reach over the table when we were dining at a restaurant and begin eating my meal before I'd touched it or he'd touched his own. Or distractedly grab *my* gym socks from the top of the laundry pile and wear them to work out and return them to me stretched as big as a wind sleeve.

We continued to pick at the breadbasket. I was trying not to be hurt, but I was hurt. The loss of toast-France had caused another little scroll to unfurl, this time with all the individual instances of his carelessness written upon it in tiny script.

"Hey. Hey. Tootsie," he whispered. "Steal some dry toasts for the trip today. Come on."

There was a basket of plastic-wrapped thick French-style melba toasts sitting on the buffet table. If we were to purchase a package at the store, they would cost approximately three dollars.

"No," I snapped.

"Please," he whined.

"No way. If you want the toasts so badly, *you* steal them. You have bigger pockets. Or we could, oh, I don't know, buy some on our way out of town? So we don't look like vagabonds?"

"Please, Tou Tou. Come on. Be my *frieeeeend*. My stomach. It hurts so much."

"No. I'm serious. You steal them your own damn self on your way out."

He widened his eyes and moaned, "But Tootsie! I can't . . . I'm not fast enough. My knee! My poor knee!!"

My father had snapped the tendons in his knee a few years ago. He'd been transplanting a birch tree from one end of the Camp's property to another, thinking it would help during mosquito season. My mother and I are extremely susceptible to their bites—the marks will swell to the size of tangerines. He'd heard some Quebec lore about birches and their mosquito-repelling capabilities. Later, it turned out he'd been misinformed. But not before he fell into the large hole he'd dug that was meant to receive the tree. After he'd walked around using golf putters as canes for a few weeks, my mother suggested he see a doctor. He'd undergone two surgeries. Technically, his knee was fine. But the accident had revealed to him that he was capable of real, mortal deterioration. His walk became more delicate. He had begun to fall, sometimes down entire sets of stairs. Especially the narrow staircase that led to his wine cellar. One day I found him at the bottom, his body as curved as a shrimp's, perfectly still save for the gentle rise and fall of his shoulder. I think it scared him. It definitely scared me.

But when my dad discovered he could pretty much get away with doing nothing physically strenuous for days on end, he began blaming his knee for all shortcomings, as a sort of sociological experiment to ascertain the relationship between people's blind goodwill and the point at which they're able to apply their skills of critical analysis to a raving cripple.

Sometimes I am convinced my father is a sociopath.

"Please, Tootsen."

"Argh. *Fine*," I huffed. I walked over to the buffet table.

"No! Not now!" he hissed.

I whipped around to face him. "Are you actually trying

to micromanage my toast-stealing technique? Are you being serious??"

"Do it at *zee* end of the meal. On our way out, like you said." He shook his head and motioned me back to the table.

We finished our water, and as we exited the breakfast room, I crammed five packages of toasts into my pockets.

"Don't crush them, Tootsie!"

Wrenching my eyelids up as far as they would go, I rolled my eyeballs at him in a sweeping, slow-motion rainbow arc. I skittered down the hall and around the corner, pretending I was being pursued by the authorities. I could tap-dance us out of this funk. When I stopped and rounded the corner to see if he was following me, to see if he was laughing at my joke, I instead saw him leaning his shoulder on the hallway's ornate cream-and-yellow wallpaper, eyes closed and heaving breath.

At the checkout desk, my father caused a thunderstorm. I caught the odd word, mostly coming from my dad, as he was the unit who was raising his voice. He was leaning over the desk in a predatory manner, eyes fixed on the hapless front desk clerk, who was clearly wishing himself dead at that particular moment. The clerk's posture indicated some godly hand had ripped out four or five of his vertebrae. I heard rumblings in French, then, (*French swear word*) "CHICKEN!" . . . (*more French swear words*), "AUDACIOUSNESS OF THE ROOM SERVICE WAITER!" . . . (*some hand-on-desk slamming*),

"MOSQUITOES!!" I sulked around the concierge desk. *Does he think this expended energy is worth it?*

It's no help that I, on the other hand, live in fear that my mistreatment of a waiter, or a salesclerk, or a taxi driver, will automatically result in that person being declared the Master of the Known Universe by some cruel (but fair) cabal and I will spend the rest of my days being fed a diet of garbage slurry and mashed-up Madagascar cockroaches, naked, while being cattle-prodded by zombie-ghosts with melting faces in bloody army attire.

My deficit of balls and spine was especially clear a while back, after I had purchased a plug-in vibrator from an upscale Toronto sex shop. One November night, I climbed into bed, sans Matthew, reached over for my electric equivalent, propped up my knees under the comforter, and flicked the switch. Immediately there was a searing heat, an incandescent blast, and a muffled popping sound. I leapt out of bed, throwing the vibrator across the room, then threw off the blanket and used a pillow to snuff out the little orange-tinged burn holes in the fitted sheet, which were spreading like islands at low tide. Save for a small singe on my upper thigh, my parts were intact, including those identifying me as a woman.

On the Internet, I found an e-mail address for the head of the crisis management team of the vibrator company and sent him a note, explaining the tragic demise of my apparatus, my sheets, my comforter, and my leg. My intent was not litigious. I just figured they should know lest it happened again. Instead of kicking off the letter with a tone that corresponded with my level of trauma (righteous indignation, drunken rage, manic distress), the first words I typed out were:

> *Dear Sir,*
> *I apologize for bothering you with such a ridiculous claim, but . . .*

After much hemming and *ehmm*ing and protestations of "Oh no, I couldn't possibly . . . ," the manager forced me to accept a two-thousand-dollar cash settlement. I used it to pay off my Visa bill and to buy a modest new vibrator that operated on double A batteries. I didn't deserve two thousand dollars for a story that ended up being a great joke to tell at baby showers. Now I fear I will suffer karmic retribution for accepting the money. I believe in karma only when it's bound to work against me. As far as I'm concerned, my karmic account has always, always been in the red. Or at least since February 2001.

A printed-out copy of the bill appeared on the mottled gray-and-white marble of the checkout counter. I watched my father sign it with a victorious flourish, his face comically stony. He jabbed the pen down at the end of his signature—a huffy punctuation that said, *It is unwise to fuck with me, my friend.* As I collected our bags, I noticed most of the staff—the other desk agents, the bellhops, one valet—were stealing glances at my father, at one another, and at me, now busily trying to gather all the luggage as though I were, in fact, my dad's aide-de-camp and not a blood relation.

He strode toward me, grinning.

"Let's go. Heheh."

"What?" I asked, averting my eyes from his like a good . . . sherpa?

"They gave us free breakfast," he said. He was delighted with himself.

"Victory for the Borels," I said somberly.

"Don't start with me," he said.

"I'm not starting with you. It's fine. I don't think your behavior is necessary sometimes."

"The chicken was not cooked. It was not cooked in the middle. It was pink."

"I know. I saw it. But there's a way of saying it without being a total assho—" I stopped myself. My father doesn't like it when I call him names like "asshole." He thinks it is disagreeable.

"I'm trying to help with the service. I am doing them a favor."

"By yelling at them about mosquitoes during mosquito season?"

"Hotels should have screens on the windows. Look at your eye, Tootsie!"

"Fine." Moderately satisfied with his violent benevolence, I dragged the luggage out to the parking lot. *The content of his complaint is correct. But the form is not.* To decompress, I threw everything into the trunk, quickly, messily, as though I were playing a psychotic game of Tetris. All the items smashed against one another and filled the back of the car.

My men. My men and their expressions of suffering. *Oh, poor me, I'm a man, and I'm suffering, and I don't know what to do. I only know how to express my suffering through belligerence and unkindness. But I love you! It doesn't take away from my love for you!*

Hours ago, I had woken up missing Matthew. I'd wanted to smell his scent. He always chose the cleanest fragrances to put all over his body. His shampoo and deodorant and pH levels married flawlessly, causing him to emit classy fragrances from his hair and flesh. Speed Stick and the lightest perspiration. When we embraced, my head fit right into the nook where his gorgeously defined shoulder met his graceful collarbone. I loved this and would breathe him in like a junkie when he brought me in for a hug. Much of our relationship revolved around commiseration—and I wondered if all the existential complaining I did was really just an excuse to bury my face safely into his armpit to smell that smell.

But Matthew punched walls. Never people, only walls. He was depressed in the same way I was depressed after my accident. The difference between us was that he was never as adept at finding the joke, and his depression seemed perennial. He didn't laugh easily at his own sadness, at the big gag that was life. So when he'd get too drunk, he'd run away from me and go on a punching rampage. Four months before this wine trip, I'd organized a dinner party at my house. Matthew had received a bad haircut that day and felt poorly about himself as a result. He could have participated in the conversations around the table, in the fetching and pouring of the wine I carefully selected, in the serving and taking away of the plates. But he was too self-conscious, too dejected. His hair became the awkward symbol of everything else that was wrong—his basement apartment, his relationships with his other friends, his insecurities about not holding a university degree and working a menial job at CBC, pushing around metal carts full of technological equipment and booking radio studios in England for the national correspondents. He eventually left, in the middle of my party, without saying good-bye. He just walked out my front door.

In the kitchen, I was topping off sundaes with crushed candied pecans and ground-up espresso beans. When I made my entrance into my dining room, proudly holding the platter of desserts, he had disappeared. I had noticed, but no one else had, so the party continued. I faked my way through the enjoyment of my sundae, the late bottle vintage Port, the absurd drunken conversation about how our lives would be different if there were tigers on the loose in the city. The following day, Matthew and I met for a late afternoon meal of sandwiches, and I saw that his right fist was swollen and scabby on the knuckles. I said, "Matty, what the . . . ?" and he said, "Uh, right. Yes. This. I left your place and put my hand through a shed in one of the alleys behind your house, on my way home." I wanted to tell him how hurt and embarrassed I'd been. How humiliating and sad it was for my boyfriend to get up and leave in the middle of a dinner party. But he was bleeding. His hand was the size of a cantaloupe—splintery and torn up. So I lined up my finger with the bridge of his nose and stroked that. Then I stroked his bruised hand until my doomed love for him returned.

I will not miss Matthew. I will drive the car to Alsace. And so I drove. We drove in silence. My father asked for the stolen toasts. I pulled the crumpled packages out of the various pockets of my army pants and asked him if he was feeling any better, better enough for our tastings. He chewed thoughtfully. He took a few more bites. This caused him to liven up for a little while. He finally nodded and said, "I think so. I think it will be fine." Relieved, I sang the opening bars to "La Mer" by Charles Trenet. He wiped the crumbs off his shirt and joined me. We didn't know any of the words beyond "*La mer . . . ,*" so we filled in the rest of the words with swooning babble: "*La mer . . . da da da daaaaa . . . da da . . . da da da da . . . da da da DA da da da DAAAAAAA da da da da da da . . . da da daaaaaa . . . da.*" We drove for several hours, taking a wrong turn and looping back, stopping every now and again for water, for antinausea pills for him and antihistamines for me. The houses on the side of the road began looking more German, as if they were made of gingerbread. Town names went from two syllables to seven syllables.

"Tootsie, pull over, please," he said.

I took my eyes off the road for one second and noticed the skin tone of my father's face. It was similar to that of wet Silly Putty.

"Oh. Fuck."

I skidded the car to a halt on the road's pebbly soft shoulder; he threw open the door and sprayed vomit all over the ferns.

I think seeing your own dad vomit is worse than seeing him cry.

As he was heaving, I resisted the urge to reach out and pat the back of his neck. No one likes to be touched in midpurge. His back contracted spasmodically, then he went slack, hanging his head between his knees. Every trace of small-child anger dissolved. I thought of him at the bottom of the cellar stairs. So helpless. My little crumpled human croissant, breathing softly, in and out.

Suddenly, he ducked back into the car, clapped his hands twice on the dashboard, *paf paf*, and said, *"Allez-hop!"* which is French for, Let's get the hell out of here!

Claude Monet had painted the dusk outside the windshield, done up in chunks of the more effeminate Crayola colors—periwinkle blue and rose and torch red and orchid. Sprawling out in front of us, it was an arresting scene. My eyes were bleary from six hours of watching asphalt and horizon. Road signs slurred by, green and white.

"Okay, Dad. We need to focus."

"The place is called Hotel Arnold. In Itterswiller," he stated robotically.

"Have you seen a sign for Itterswiller?" I asked.

"No," he said.

"Look on the map."

"It's not on the map."

"Um . . ."

"I have other directions," he offered.

"Perfect."

"Did we pass Barr?"

"I don't know."

"Take a left."

I turned.

"Now what?" I clamped my teeth together. The anger crept back inside me.

"Look for the sign for Andlau."

"I can't see anything. You're supposed to be looking, re-member? You're the navigator."

"Tootsie, it's too dark. I am sick."

"Well, I don't have night vision, you know. And I know you're sick. I'm sorry that you're sick. But I have to keep my eyes on the road. I mean, my eye. I can't even see out of the other eye. You don't even care, do you? About my eye?"

"Don't talk to me like that. I am your father. I do care about your eye."

"I KNOW YOU ARE MY FATHER. I wasn't talking to you like anything. I just need you to find the sign." I was losing my patience again. I couldn't be expected to carry all the bags and hold all the buckets all the time.

"Opppppss!" My dad has hybridized "oops" and "*hop!*" It's his way of saying, "You just screwed up."

"Did I just screw up?" I asked.

"You passed the exit for Andlau."

"Thanks. Great. Do you want me to turn the car around?" I snapped.

"Do whatever you want."

"YOU CAN'T TELL ME I'M WRONG, THEN TELL ME WHAT TO DO, THEN SHUT DOWN WHEN I ASK YOU FOR HELP."

His eyes pointed straight up, as though he were trying to locate his eyebrows. He said nothing.

I made a brisk, graceless three-point turn, almost backing into a vineyard. They were all around us, the vines. They looked like gnarled old wooden hands clawing out of the brittle grass, ready to grab small children.

"There's a sign for Andlau."

"That's good, right?"

"Yes. Take two." He said "Take two" like "That's the game," with many extra A's. "*Taaaaaake* two!"

"Tell me what I'm supposed to do next, so I don't screw it up again."

"*Au rond-point, prendre la deuxième sortie D35.*" He was reading directions from the back of the itinerary.

"So I'll see the sign for the D35 at the next roundabout."

"This is the plan."

Tentatively, my foot hovered over the accelerator. I curved around the roundabout in short, slow bursts, waiting for my father to yell out the next direction. He would yell, "Ah!" My shoulders were in a stress shrug of anticipation.

"AH!"

"This is the exit?"

"That is the exit."

The Citroën's headlights flashed over a white sign with a word on it that spelled v-i-c-t-o-r-y.

I-T-T-E-R-S-W-I-L-L-E-R.

"Awesome."

"We are not there yet."

"Why do you have to be so ominous? This town is tiny. Piece of cake. Hotel Arnold, right?"

"You are on the wrong road."

"How many goddamn roads does this town have?"

"Ah, Tootsie, that's enough, *hein*? *Langage, s'il te plaît!*" His tone was a knife.

"Fine. FINE. What road am I supposed to be on?"

"Route des Vins."

"And what road am I on?"

"Route Epfig."

"But is this a road in Itterswiller, or have I driven out of town?"

"Turn the car around."

"Oh, *now* you're the great and all-knowing navigator? NOW?"

"Turn."

"Have I passed through Itterswiller or what?"

"Turn the car."

The road was the width of a yoga mat; my three-point turn was a thirty-eight-point turn. My skull was so hot, I was convinced my eyeballs would turn to jelly and ooze out my sockets. Leagues beyond frustrated, I jerked the shift around the gearbox violently and bashed my boot alternately into the brake, clutch, and accelerator.

"Take it easy, Tootsen." He'd sandpapered the edges off his voice. His words were an olive branch. Smaller. An olive twig. But it was enough. I felt a tiny explosion of relief in my chest, allowing me to release more breath than I had been able to for the last hour.

"All right. We're almost there. I can smell it. So, we go straight?"

"Yes, Tootsen."

Route Epfig miraculously turned into Route des Vins.

"Yesssss . . ." I sighed.

Dinner was cordial. I was tired, he was sick, so we were quiet. My face was a pulsating mass—I'd forgotten to buy balm for my cold sore at the pharmacy. If stuck with a ballpoint pen, it would explode. In the hotel's tidily rustic dining room, he ate plain rice while I stabbed around at my vegetables. They were well buttered and rolled elusively over the plate. *Isn't this supposed to be the time of our lives? Shouldn't his face be in soft focus? Today provided no material for a montage scene. Dah dah dah! We are driving! Oh yeah . . . Here we go! To the place! And the other place! Smiles and laughs! His past, my past, here's the metaphor, emotional similarities: Oh, you do that, too? I thought I was the only one!*

I was waving my fork in the air, languidly following a fly

that was buzzing around the discarded leftovers from our *amuse-bouches*: tiny chunks of salami on mini sunflower-seed buns. I smashed the fork into the table whenever it settled on an item that would not break.

"How are you feeling as of right now?"

"Oh, up and down, Tootsie. You know."

"And what if you can't drink anything?"

"Then I don't drink anything."

"But how will I learn?" What I meant was, *How will I learn about you?*

"I don't know."

He shook his head a bit and pushed the plate away, then caught the waiter's eye and looped his wrist around twice.

"L'addition, s'il vous plaît?"

In my room, the MTV show *Pimp My Ride* was on television. In German. Xzibit, a Detroit-born rapper with angry eyes and cornrows, was asking his car-pimping colleague what it would take to adequately "pimp" a teenage girl's old rattletrap of a car. I tried to follow along, but I couldn't, despite my two years of university German.

I fell asleep hoping tomorrow would be easier to decipher than this show.

At eighty-thirty, I was woken up by some crows. I rolled out of bed and walked to the window to shout at them. I opened my mouth, but the scene below was too serene to be upset with my shouting. White morning sky, layers of rolling hills, lush and stem green and dark green and misty blue, a tall beige farmhouse, its cheery rusty-colored roof

and black cutout windows staring at me like cute square cartoon eyes.

"CAW! CAW CAW!" said the crows. They were hiding
in the Christmas trees. The trees in Alsace all look as if they
should be in the living rooms of giants, in December.

I put my hands on my hips and answered them in a scream
whisper: "CAW, CAW, jerks."

At breakfast, my questions were conceived by the Clash.
They were troublesome. 1. Should we stay or should we go?
2. Should we stay or should we go *now*?

I couldn't do this without him. And staring into his cloudy
eyes told me I likely would not be doing it with him.

"What's the deal? Are we on today or what?"

"Yes, we're going."

"Good. Great! So you'll taste with me?" Relief.

"We'll see."

"We'll see?"

"Yes, that's what we'll do. See. We will see."

My dad rose and hovered over me. He pursed his lips and
squeezed out a wide teardrop of spit.

I looked up at him. "I dare you."

The spit space between the bottom of the tear and his
pursed lips grew longer and longer.

"Don't. Don't don't don't. I don't dare you anymore."

Right before the dribble hit my ice water, he reached out
and deftly caught the blob. He cackled and wiped it on his
jeans. What was he thinking? Where was his sense of *deco-
rum*? Where had he put it? Would he find it again in Rémy

Gresser's cellar? I shook off my nervousness. This is what I love about this guy. About us. We fake spit on each other. That's our thing. Team Borel.

"Let's get this show on the road," he said.

"There is no doubt. You are a show."

"Oh yeah? I *theenk* you are a show," he said.

And so we left the hotel, put our show in the car, and took it on the road.

chapter six

We were to meet Rémy Gresser at ten-thirty. My heart was racing the way it had on the plane after those sips of bog-water wine. I stumbled confusedly over my reasons for being in that car, on this road. *Death. Dad. Chemistry. Wine.* Layered on top of my anxiety to conjure real feelings for the wines we would taste was the realization that I'd actually never been to a professional tasting in my adult life. *What's the protocol? What questions to ask? When to spit and when to swallow? What if the wine is corked and I look like an idiot again? How much am I even supposed to talk?* At the breakfast table, I'd thought about my complex love for Peter, years ago, and how at first I'd kept it to myself, conspiratorially. Weeks went by as I'd stabilized my core and strengthened my tongue enough to form the Three Big Words. Much of me was afraid that the words and feelings wouldn't match up, and once they were uttered, they'd no longer be applicable. They'd somehow sound wrong and just flop around like suffocating fish and die. Finally, one night, when we were lying in bed about to go to sleep, I felt him twitch. When I looked over at him, I saw his eyes were locked on the ceiling and wide as moons. He began to scavenge nervously for words. He was making half sentences, quarter sentences. He'd stop and start again. After a minute or two, I realized it was a preface, the preface I needed. I blurted, "I know, I love you, too." Then we both began laughing hysterically. My words had curled up into him perfectly. We built our love out of language, and it was a grand and beautiful home.

But then the accident happened, and all the words we invented turned into those awkward flapping fish.

What if the same thing happens today?

Over breakfast, I'd mentally noted a brigade of unconventional wine descriptors. *Develop a language framework, like you did with Peter.* My father had always loathed the standard fruits-and-vegetables descriptions for wine. He thinks pairings are a sham and snorts at those who propagate old wine snob clichés ("ABC—anything but Chardonnay!" or "I only love big jammy Australian Shiraz!"). As I had been systematically annihilating the pastry basket, I'd been thinking of pastry-related words that could also apply to wine, maybe, depending on the wine. Flaky. Doughy. Fragrant. Pointy. Spongy. Ephemeral. Airy. Golden. Delicious. Croissant-y. Icing-stuck-to-the-plastic-top-of-freezer-aisle cakey. I moved on to adjectives for tannins, not knowing exactly what they were. *Tannins. Red wine has tannins, but I actually have not a hot clue what they are. In a tasting, tannins always come up. People say, "Smooth tannins . . ." "Broad tannins . . ." I should prepare a sentence including this word. Does white wine have tannins?*

My father stared out the window, and I watched his eyes flicker lazily from left to right and left to right and left to right as he watched the Alsatian Christmas trees zip by on their yellow grassy carpets.

"Does white wi—" I stopped myself. This question was stupid, I was sure of it. This question would disappoint him.

"Huh?"

"No. No, nothing. I was going to ask you something, but I answered my own question. Carry on." I had not answered my own question, but it was probably one of those questions that would be answered for me, in time, if I kept quiet and observed the interactions between my father and the viticulturists, and my father and the wine. *That is, if he participates. If he participates, I will employ this perceptive process of elimination.*

As we drove into Gresser's tiny town of Andlau, a Ferrari hurtled by, spraying the side of our Picasso with dust that went *clink clink clink.* I yelped; he sighed.

"How can you buy a yellow Ferrari?" he said with exasperation, hand clutching his stomach.

"Dad, can you keep on the lookout for Route de l'École, please?"

"Only a sick person buys a yellow Ferrari," he responded.

"We're late," I said. My nerves were tingling.

"I know."

By the time we pulled up to the Gressers' low-roofed L-shaped house, made of gray stones, moist and shiny from an early morning shower, we were one hour and twenty minutes late. I slammed the car door and saw that beyond the house were vines, endless rows of vines, ascending up, up, up, like lines of calm, patient millionaires waiting to pick up their opera tickets at the box office. The ones in the distance were tiny dots. Where the dots ended, the heavy, eroded slope of the Vosges Mountains began, lush and green. Their old, eroded crests met with the sky, smoky with cloud.

"Bonjour!" a disembodied voice called. Immediately, a hairy, goofy-looking mutt began barking salutations, bouncing up and down—as if on a pogo stick—within a wire mesh enclosure. A big, rugged man emerged from the house, wearing a light blue short-sleeved button-up shirt and gray work pants. He looked like a kindly bus driver. He had a nose a little like a fingerling potato and droopy lips. His French was accented with a German singsong. The ends of his sentences were all melodic questions.

"Les Borels? Bienvenue. Rémy Gresser." He smiled, obviously indifferent to our botched arrival time. My three-tiered panic about being loathed by this man for disrespecting him by being late—as well as being nervous about feelings and language, as *well* as my ill father—was downgraded to a familiar, straightforward panic about the two latter anxieties.

"*Philippe Borel. Ma fille, Kathryn,*" my father introduced us.

"*Je suis journaliste!*" I exclaimed moronically. I'd intended to convey some sort of general credibility and to remind myself that language and understanding were never so far out of reach. I sounded like a talking doll with a pull string. *Math is hard!*

"*Ah! Très bien!*" Remy nodded and continued to smile. I flushed and picked a woolen ball off the sleeve of my sweater.

He led us through the gate, through a door, and down to his cellar. I breathed in a cobweb.

"How long have you been doing this?" I asked, coughing away the clingy filaments. My French felt clunky. *Incorrect conjugation!* My question drooped in the air. *God, it sounds like I'm trying to pick him up.*

"Oh, a while. I'm a direct descendant of Eberhard Gresser. He began making wine in 1575. I'm the thirteenth gen-eration." He was uncorking the row of green bottles, sleek and feminine, the shapes of stretched-out bowling pins. *Four hundred and thirty years.*

"Wah-ooh," I wowed in French.

"Did you feel like you had a choice in the matter?" I tried to make my intonation sound light and innocuous, but with a trace of solemnity, in order to leave open the possibility for this kind man to break down on my shoulder and sob about the true passion that slipped through his fingers long ago . . . Artisan chocolate maker? Pediatric oncologist? Pilot?

Steeplechase jockey? *Are these the right questions to be asking?*
I'm being too personal. I should ask about his family of bottles.
People love talking about their children.

"I didn't ask myself the question, you know, of whether I
wanted to do something else. It was the only life I wanted.
On est maître chez soi. Sit down, please." He motioned toward
the bench, where my father had already sat down, now with
both hands splayed out, in a pain trance. I wondered if he
would vomit. I hoped he wouldn't. In the corner of my eye,
I could see his hairy fingers, the skin taut from his flat grip
on the table. *Don't vomit. Don't do it. Don't mess this up. Don't*
mar the bouquet of the wines.

The labels on the bottles read as follows, left to right:

Duttenberg 2004. Riesling.
Moenchberg 1999. Riesling. Grand Cru.
Weibelsberg 2002. Riesling.
Kastelberg 2003. Riesling.
Weibelsberg 1985. Riesling.
Weibelsberg 1997. Riesling.
Moenchberg 2000. Riesling.

I didn't need my father for this. I could decipher what
the labels meant. Duttenberg, Kastelberg, Moenchberg, and
Weibelsberg referred to the towns in which the vineyards
were located. Riesling was the grape from which the wine
was made. The years were the years in which the grapes

were grown. Grand Cru meant the wine had been given a special classification for its superior quality.

"What soils are they grown in?"

Rémy blasted through a list of soils in his pretty accent, da da DA, da da DA, and that's all it sounded like to me, da da DA. *Oh Christ. The 2004 Duttenberg was grown in* argile. *What's the translation for that? Clay? The Grand Cru in* calcaire *something, something about fossils and* calcaire, *which is calcium. Calcium? No. Calcium dirt? Nonsense. I'm translating wrong. I'm going as fast as I can. What's* gres des Vosges? Grès *. . . granite? Why did I ask about DIRT, of all things? I only did passably in that section of grade 8 geography, when we studied the Canadian shield and I got kicked out of class for attempting to endear myself to my fellow classmates—I was once again the new kid, this time in Quebec City—by doing what I thought was a really funny impression of a person with Down syndrome.* Now Rémy was on about the region of Alsace having relatively liberal legislation. *What does that mean? Compared to who?*

"I'll go get you some bread," Rémy said. He left the room.

"Did you get that stuff about the soil?" I asked my father nervously.

"No. I wasn't listening."

He was swirling the first wine. I mimicked him, swirling the second one. I sniffed it and tasted. He sniffed his and put the glass back down on the table.

"I can't," he said, "I'm too sick."

I swallowed and tried the next one. There was no spittoon, and we—rather, I—had seven wines to get through.

"Dad."

"What."

"I can't drink all these. I'm going to be hammered."

"Then spit them out."

"There's nowhere for me to spit."

"Spit on the floor, that's why it's unfinished."

"On the floor?" I inspected the floor for evidence of others' vinous dribbles.

"Yes. This is the traditional thing to do."

"I don't feel comfortable doing that."

"Try it."

Forcing the wine to the front of my mouth, I squeezed my lips together. It gushed all down my chin and onto my sweater. Humiliated, I turned away from him and wiped my face with my sleeve.

"Am I supposed to finish the wine in the glasses?"

"You can if you want."

Rémy reentered. He asked us what we thought.

"*Très raffiné*," my father said definitively.

"*Merci, monsieur.*"

"It has a nose like gasoline a bit, doesn't it? *Comme le pétrole,*" he continued. I was full of envy and curiosity. *Gasoline!*

"*Exacte, Monsieur Borel.*"

Rémy then looked at me. I smiled and nodded and stared at the third glass in the row, trying to disengage. The only emotion I had was impending tipsiness.

Rémy explained the variety of wines he had laid out for us: *"Je fais des vins pour chaque instant."* He tried to make a wine for every instant, for every occasion. He said there were easy wines, ones that required no concentration. But sometimes he liked to concentrate on wine. These were his meditation wines. I nodded some more and drank wines four, five, and six. I couldn't tell which ones were his meditation wines. I was meditating on what words I should be saying. What words I should have been stringing together into meaningful sentences. Nothing. I had nothing.

My father pushed one of the glasses forward and drummed his fingers along its base.

"This one is exceptional. It's . . . it's . . ." He held up his finger and drew a straight, quick horizontal line through the air and made a *sssssst!* noise. "It's so clean. Almost like licking a stone. Fresh, full of minerals."

"Oui, oui!"

Both men were now smiling at each other. They chatted more about the meditation wines. I became lost.

"What do you think, Tou Tou? These are great, *hein*?" my father asked. He was fighting through his cramps for me, eager to engage.

"Mmm-hmm. I definitely caught a whiff of minerals. And yes, gasoline. That, too," I lied.

"You've got the palate, Toots."

No, I don't. I felt annoyed and ashamed.

My father scratched some brief and illegible notes in his

leather-bound Day-Timer and snapped the thing shut savagely with a *thhhppt*.

"It's touching, that you're taking this trip together," Rémy said, fixing his careful eyes on me and my father. "Wine is pleasure," he said, "and doing this with family must be a pleasure, too."

I glanced at my father, who was back to clawing at the table and his wasted gut.

I finished wine number seven. The cellar became brighter and strangely defined. The color palette of the room changed. The shadows seemed darker; the air fell on me like damp hand towels. I attempted to make my Face of Intense Contemplation, by crinkling my brow ever so slightly, pulling up my chin at a twenty-degree angle, and seizing the left corner of my mouth. I hoped it made me seem as though I were thinking hard, and this thinking was of such complexity and unattainable truth that I was slightly annoyed at myself (which I was, for other reasons).

As Rémy cleared the glasses, I searched for the keys to the car.

"You're okay to drive, Tou Tou?" My father's voice was weak. He stared at the upper corners of the walls within Rémy's cellar, back and forth, head lolling slightly, his eyes registering nothing, his lips saying nothing, his body stooped and concave. It was like watching a piece of industrial machinery power down for the night. A piece of industrial machinery that is outfitted with an LED display that powers on automatically when the machine powers down and a message that scrolls, "YOU ARE ON YOUR OWN. YOU ARE ON YOUR OWN. YOU ARE ON YOUR OWN. YOU ARE ON YOUR OWN . . ."

Outside in the fresh soggy air, I trapped Rémy's right hand in both of mine and shook it hard, feigning radical delight.

"*Merci, merci, Monsieur Gresser. Merci infiniment! Merci!*" I said psychotically.

"*De rien, Kathryn, Monsieur Borel. Un plaisir. Bonne chance.*"

Dutifully, I placed myself behind the wheel, even though I should not have been driving. But I wanted to FLY to the second tasting. I wanted my father to ask me the same questions so that I could think harder and try harder and give him truthful responses. I wished I could tell him that I was afraid to drive and that I hadn't tasted any minerals in that Riesling. And that I was afraid of no higher common language emerging from our special trip. Panicking, I fumbled the key around the ignition, clattering it against the plastic and metal until it found its way inside. We took off.

But the day will be okay. The day will get better. It must eventually end up in the general vicinity of "okay." We have two other tastings. Two new opportunities to accentuate the positive and eliminate the negative!

Breathe.

"How late are we?" I asked.

"One hour and a half," he responded.

"Oh Christ."

"Why are you upset?"

I avoided the question. "Where are we going?"

"I don't know. Toots, why are you crying?"

"Can you check the map?" I answered.

"Yes."

"Can you check the map now?" I snipped.

"Yesssss."

"So. The town is called . . ."

"Zeeven-blech Oval."

"Huh?"

"Jeeven-black Oh-Vale."

"What?"

He was mumbling. He righted himself and tightened his jaw. "DeefenBACK o-VALL!" He fired off the name like a German general.

"Spell it."

"D-I-E-F-F-E-N-B-A-C-H A-U V-A-L."

"Oh. Okay. Which way?"

"I don't know."

I went around the same roundabout three times. I was dizzy. All the towns looked the same. We were lost in another farming community, with the same fields and the same animals and the same quiet houses, gray and cold, no one on the identical streets. I drove up a gravel road. It was a dead end. There were no people, just mist and sodden grass and soccer pitches. This went on forever. Forever and ever. My tears flowed harder. I thought of how the old man had looked, lying on the highway, and how it had been so similar to my father's position at the bottom of his cellar stairs after he'd fallen down them so hard and fast.

"Whose vineyard are we visiting, anyway?" My voice wiggled around. I needed to maintain. *Maintain maintain maintain. Be the road. Be the car. Be the vineyards. Be the grapes. Breathe.*

"It's not a vineyard," my father said. He'd stopped asking me why I was crying.

"What do you mean, it's not a vineyard?"

"We are doing an eaux-de-vie tasting."

"Eaux-de-vie."

"Eaux-de-vie, yes."

"Like, the hard alcohol."

"Exactly."

"But . . . WHY?"

The tears reached a critical mass and came spilling out, drenching my cheeks in hot rivulets, pooling at my chin, dropping off onto my sweater, forming a puddle on the thin wool covering my chest, then sliding en masse onto my lap. Like my pants, this day was mess.

When we got to Dieffenbach-au-Val, we were two hours late in meeting Manou Massenez, a gorgeous, sleek woman in her late forties wearing a suit of heather blue that had been made by angels. She was stunning and sweet and toured us around the Massenez distillery, where her family had been making fruit brandies since 1870. We went into the bowels of the operation, where the pressed fruits were heated up, where the aromas were squeezed out and steamed and cooled and condensed and transformed into deadly potent liqueur. And she was so gracious, and my cold sore was bleeding again, and I was fighting back more tears because none of this was what I expected. How could my father and I do this every day for the next fifteen days if I was not talented and if we kept getting lost amid roving bands of goats and kept tasting liquid that was not wine while my father vomited all over France's beautiful countryside? And why was I panicking in this country-side, on a trip that I was so lucky to be on, so lucky with my dear father and this dazzling woman who was rack-ing up twenty-four shot glasses of different eaux-de-vie—waters-of-life—which were doing exactly what the name promised, giving me life, giving me new life so that I was not very sad anymore and certainly no longer felt like crying, because the eaux-de-vie were 100 proof? And so this water of life carried us into the woodsy little auberge that looked like something out of *The Chronicles of Narnia,* where a blurry-faced waiter served me foie gras and boar with blackberry sauce *avec* endless glasses of clean, light red wine, which I drank while my father ate plain spaetzle until it was gone. And when it was gone, someone was signing the bill and suddenly we were saying good-bye to Manou Massenez, who had just given me a tube of special balm for my bleeding cold sore, for which I hugged her emotionally and turned and stepped into the car, cross-eyed but hiding it from my sick, dying father because I wanted to take care of him not only now, but for the rest of his life or mine or time.

As the tears returned, I turned to him and said, "Please, Dad. No more for today."

And he said, "I know, Tootsie. I will call to cancel the next tour. But first, please drive up the road. I have to vomit."

This time I didn't even try to reach out and pat him on the back. I just sat there, my heart mute and paralyzed.

chapter seven

There was a knock at my door. The time was seven o'clock
or minus sixty-seven o'clock or some time that was very
early—too early for him to be here, bugging me to get up,
to join him for breakfast, more toast, more embarrassing
nonbuttered crumby toast that will burst and spread crispy
shrapnel all over his stubbly chin, crumbs I would have to
dust off with a napkin because he didn't notice. Like he
didn't notice as I faked and fumbled through all of yesterday.
I pulled open the door. He was smiling eerily. Inexplicably,
he was Mister Golden Sun. His brightness was invading my
gloomy, guilty sleepiness. I wanted nothing to do with him.
Last night I had made up nervous dreams, had woken up
frequently to scratch at my viciously itchy right arm. These
were my anxious physical crosses to bear—the ugly mani-
festations of the contents of my skull. Stress-induced cold

sores and a condition my naturopath describes as "phantom itching." My arm was bleeding. My father was smiling. I was heavy. Every molecule of my body was weighted with a drop of mercury, attached by a short gossamer line of good-quality fishing tackle.

"Why are you here bothering me?" I folded my arms high and tight across my chest, so that my fingers were grasping the outside of my shoulder blades. I bitchily wondered why he hadn't pushed me harder for elaborate answers to his questions: during the tasting, while I was losing my mind in the car. I was reminded of his searching face after he'd tried to reanimate the dead old man. "The man you keeled. He was eighty-three. He was a pharmacist. I have made you some fish." *I don't like fish! Why didn't he know how to talk to me properly?! His sensitivities are all crossed! He throws analysis at me when I need comfort and comfort when I need analysis!* I tugged at my shoulder blades and flexed my biceps to seem tough.

"Tootsie. Sweet, poor, sensitive Tootsie. Good news," he said.

"Hmm. What?"

"It is finished. The sickness. I have not vomited for . . ." He began counting on his fingers, then ran out of fingers. "Many hours. The stomach is good. I can begin eating garbage again. I am good. We are good. Everything is good." He smiled and hit me with a double thumbs-up.

Letting go of my shoulders, I stuck my palms up and out for a tentative high ten. He wound up, and swooped his arm toward me, smacking his hand against mine along the way.

I can bounce back from things. I have medium-to-high bounce-back capabilities. They used to be better, quicker, bouncier. For a while, after the accident, they were buried under six hundred tons of landfill garbage. But they're still around.

"And we should maybe drop some appointments, too, *hein?*" he added.

My dad was with It. He got It. He's the heavyweight champion of It. We were back. *This trip is not going to Shop-Vac my soul out of my very core, it will not cause our relationship to morph into a landscape of nuclear winter. Likely not. It is not likely that I will come into contact with a Shop-Vac for my soul and, later, a landscape of nuclear winter. I have never believed in absolutes.*

My father sat on the bed and picked up the telephone. "How many should I cancel, Tootsie?" he asked.

"You're the expert. What about half? I don't know. Don't cancel the ones where we get into the vineyards," I said, thinking about my dirt question to Rémy Gresser. *Maybe if I can plunge my hand into that dirt, into the roots, this stuff will come to life.*

I shuffled around the room, picking items up and putting them down. I flicked a light switch on and off. *Maybe if I see the grapes, the actual grapes, I'll understand the transformation. Like when you meet a baby and see how their vague personality traits—the way they chuckle, their aversion to raisins but not currants—will become amplified and crystallized in later life. I want to meet the babies. Wine babies.* I flicked the light on and off again. My father and I had a nice bonding moment over a human baby, once, in California. Nico was working in San Francisco for a

boutique company that designed websites to make corpora-
tions like Nike seem as though they were interested in art.
My dad was keen on tooling around some of Sonoma's vineyards, I was keen on perpetrating a tan while eating large
bowls of comped Caesar salad poolside. We drove north and
stayed in the Fairmont Hotel there. The director of the hotel's operations, Matt Sterne, had worked with my father
when he was younger—he was a protégé of sorts.

When we visited, we all had a drink in the hotel lobby
with Matt, his blond wife, and their fresh baby. The baby
was being passed around like a spliff; my father and I both
declined when she came our way. I was sitting on my hands,
silently battling the social vertigo I tend to experience
around babies and animals—knowing that I have the power
to change the course of my entire life by following through
on one deranged impulse. The words *Don't pick up the baby
and throw it against the wall* had just begun scrolling through
my head, like the ticker at the bottom of the CNN screen.
Moments later, my father leaned over to whisper in my ear.

"Tootsie," he said.

"Hmm?" I replied.

"Do you ever get the feeling that you just want to take a
baby and kick it across the room and watch it smash against
the wall?"

It was a beautiful moment.

I looked at him fondly as he flipped to the glossary of
phone numbers at the back of the itinerary. He perched his
glasses on the bridge of his nose and dialed the first number.

He dialed and chatted and thanked and apologized, then ran his pen along the itinerary, crossing off names. With every drag of ink that appeared on the page, my chest sagged with relief. We would slow down. I would take stock. I would take stock and have time to take notes. I would remove the corks from my ears and absorb.

When he was finished, he threw the itinerary at my head again. This time he missed and the document dropped at my feet. "There you go, Toots." I lifted it and read the name of the winery at which we were expected. Recognizing the name, I exclaimed, "I know one thing!"

My father took off his glasses and rubbed his eyes. "You know more than one thing. You know many things," he responded.

"Yes, I *do*," I said in violent agreement. I'd seen bottles from this winery on liquor store shelves. I couldn't remember whether I liked this wine, but I knew it. I even knew the typeface that was used on the label. *I know two things!* The typeface was Palatino. Or something like it. I didn't know exactly. *I know one and a half things!* But I knew it was akin to a wide, bold Palatino. I even knew when I last became intoxicated on this wine: at a fake Italian restaurant where the chef had overcooked the seafood and the pappardelle components of my seafood pappardelle. A friendly acquaintance was spending her evening complaining to me about her condominium association and how they were demanding she paint her expensive plantation shutters white, because all street-facing units' windows were to look identical. This winery was vital in providing my mind with a slippery layer of alcoholic lubricant, so that anything this woman told me about plantation shutters was unable to achieve a permanent toehold. By the end of the meal, I was so drunk that the pasta was a joy to eat. *Perhaps I will thank the winery's president for this! Perhaps not.*

—◠

The fifty-kilometer drive from the minivillage of Dieffenbach-au-Val to the more southern minivillage of Riquewihr—where our target winery, Pfaffenheim, was located—was a delight. A golden green, pastoral, sunshowered delight. We did not let ourselves become distracted by trisyllabic German town names that threatened to throw us off course at any moment: Ammerschwihr, Ingersheim, Wintzenheim, Wettolsheim, Eguisheim. No, we blasted right by those signs with my father lucid, mindful, eagle-eyed, and tracing the colored map printout with his hairy finger like a Paris–Dakar rally pro. We managed not to veer into Germany or Switzerland; we stayed right inside the boundaries of France. He did not moan or convulse, and there was absolutely no pulling over of the car for him to coat the Alsatian countryside with gut brew. It was amazing. We were laughing, entertaining ourselves with fake stories about our childhood accomplishments.

"Tou Tou, you know, when I was a child, I was a composer."

"For real?"

"Yes. When I was just six, I wrote *zees* composition. Da da da DUH, da da da DUH."

He sang the opening bars of Beethoven's Fifth.

"Wow. Dad. Duly impressed. I had no idea you were behind that piece of music. Well done. What do you think about this—I wrote this song with a friend of mine when I was about eight."

Again, I sang "La Mer," with all the da da das instead of real words.

"I was under the impression that this song was by Charles Trenet."

"Oh, well, yeah, see, that was the problem. Charles and I wrote it together, but when the time came to record it, he passed it off as his own."

"How miserable," he said, concerned.

"Life's a real whore sometimes."

"True. So true."

"Painting was also a forte of mine."

"You don't say."

"My best work was of a landscape at night, a starry night; my technique was to apply thick, swirling coats of oil paint . . ."

Somehow this game kept us enthralled for the duration of the trip. By the time we pulled into the parking lot at the Pfaffenheim headquarters, we were relaxed and bleating laughter with big open mouths. A dribble of saliva cascaded off my lower lip and down my neck. My father noticed and clamped his paw on my chin, swiping away the drool and rubbing it on his pant leg. I clamped my hand over his whole face, pressing the meaty part of my hand into his nose until it squished, then bolted out of the car before he could retaliate. I ran over to his door and did a little jig. He got out and stretched.

"Pull it together," he said, and cuffed me upside the head.

"Ow. Too hard." I took a boxing stance and punched him downward, on the edge of his scapula.

"Heh. Good punch. Solid. *Ow-shh*," he said. French for ouch.

When we were escorted into his office, Alex Heinrich—the general manager of Pfaffenheim—was on the phone. His assistant, a nameless, jumpy man in his early forties, wearing a snappy gray suit, ushered us into plush wingback chairs and proceeded to stare unflinchingly at my chest. I looked down at it, making sure there was no moisturizing cream or coffee or breakfast pieces on it. I was clean. I looked back up at the jumpy man quizzically. My father's eyes were ping-ponging back and forth between my face and the face of the man who was fixated on his daughter's chest. On each person's face was a smile. Jumpy Man's was aroused, mine was pinched, my father's was amused, with a slight trace of Schadenfreude. Normal fathers—fathers who barbecue in King of the Grill aprons—would assumedly be moved to say something vaguely threatening in a situation like this. Not mine. I wonder if his entrench-ment in certain Old World values makes him appreciate these humiliating moments; maybe he regards them as a tonic for the soul.

Five hour-minutes passed, and finally Mr. Heinrich—a puckish silver-haired man with a perfect furry arc of a mustache—clunked the handset down in its cradle and apologized for the call.

"Bienvenue!" Heinrich's merry greeting snapped Jumpy Man out of his boob trance.

"Did you have trouble finding us?" he asked.

"Non," I said.

"Pas du tout," my father echoed.

Heinrich asked where we'd been yesterday.

"Chez Rémy Gresser," I answered.

"Et alors? Ça c'est bien passé?" He wanted to know how it went. He'd directed the question at me. My father, respectful, waited for me to respond. I flushed and paused, suddenly nervous again. I could feel Jumpy Man's eyes all over me.

"His wines taste like gas!" I exclaimed. *How did my father make gasoline sound like an attribute?*

Heinrich stared at me for a beat, then motioned toward the door. *"On est prêt a commencer?"*

I tailed Heinrich's car through quaint yellow-and-red Riquewihr. We parked in front of a short stone enclosure, facing a château atop a hill that was flanked on all sides by long rows of curly vines, heavy with black and violet clusters.

Alex Heinrich weaved his short body deftly in and out of the plants, plucking ripe berries and putting them into my hand. He seemed to recognize on what level I was operating. *His wines taste like gas!* I wrinkled my nose at myself and peered at my handful of purplish red orbs.

"Mange ça," he urged.

I obeyed, popping them one by one with my mouth, piercing them with my left canine so the honeyed juice trickled out slowly, like air from a floppy, pin-pricked balloon.

"What do you taste?" He waved his hands around like a symphony conductor.

"Le sucre et les fleurs." This, I was sure of. Sugar and flowers.

"Tell me the grape," he ordered.

I looked over at my dad, who was keeping one eye on me and one eye on Jumpy Man. I caught Jumpy Man's gaze; it had moved down to my ass—a rookie's move. *Doesn't he know the rules? You steal a glimpse when a girl looks away and make sure to take your eyes off the prize when the girl is on her way back to make more eye contact. Simple.*

"Kathryn?" Alex Heinrich had his eyes where they were supposed to be: on my face.

"Ah. Oui . . . Je crois . . . Gewurztraminer?" I was almost positive it was a Gewurztraminer grape. Almost.

"Bien fait."

A correct answer! Buoyed, I marched over to a higher row of vines to find a different grape to taste and identify correctly to further confirm the measure of my latent oenological prowess.

After plucking one that was bluish black, I inspected the skin. I rubbed off the thin film of dust and split it open so that its slick, pale jade insides burst forth, then shoved the thing on the end of my tongue. Again it was sweet, but more discreetly so than the Gewurztraminer, with an acidic bite that made the edges of my tongue curl inward. I did the math: We were in Alsace, it was not a region where a lot of red wine is produced, the local red wine I'd noticed on the wine list during our lunch with Manou Massenez was Pinot Noir, *noir* in French is black, and this grape was black as all hell.

"*Celui-ci, c'est du Pinot Noir?*"

"*Oui, c'est bien ça, du Pinot Noir,*" Alex Heinrich confirmed. My father was not paying attention anymore; it was elementary stuff, this juvenile game of grape identification. He was absentmindedly picking berries off another Pinot Noir vine and vacuuming them into his mouth, which he'd formed into the O shape of a perfect berry-size suction machine.

"*PINOT NOIR,*" I repeated loudly, hoping to make my father's ears prick up.

Mr. Heinrich's cell phone buzzed; he took the call. I lobbed a grape toward my dad, and it hit him in the back of the head.

"Hey," I said.

"*Aieee,*" he said.

"I get it. Are you seeing me get it?"

"Yes, I see that." He held out his hand for a high five. I smacked it.

"And I just figured out tannins, eating those Pinot Noir berries."

"You know what tannins are."

"Well, no. Kind of. Not really. But I do know. Now, I

mean. They're what gives a red wine its structure. It's in the skins. Tannins come from the skins."

"Its skeleton comes from the skins," he said.

"Yes, whatever, its skeleton. Sure. The bones. If it had no bones, it wouldn't stand up. It would just be a big floppy mess. I could feel it on the sides of my face with the Pinot Noir, but not with the Gewurztraminer."

"Do you know why?"

"Sure. Of course."

I paused. I didn't actually know.

"Wait. No. I don't actually know," I said. Yesterday, it was the question I'd dared not ask. Today, we were allied again.

"Red wine gets its shape from . . ."

"The skins of the grapes."

"And white wine gets *eets* shape from . . ."

"Not the skins of the grapes."

"*Vahree* good."

"So . . ."

"From the acidity of the fruit," he encouraged.

"Ah. Right." This was basic architecture. *Skins and acidity help build reds and whites like good, intuitive language helps build real feelings.* I was going to share this with my father, but Heinrich reappeared at my side, gesticulating.

"You have to understand that the Alsacian microclimate makes it the driest winegrowing region in France."

I smelled the air and put my face into the sun, breathing in the strawlike grass and the chocolate brown earth and the vegetable scents emanating from the vines. *All of this is architecture.*

He pointed up to the Vosges Mountains and explained how they form a protective barrier for the region.

"The summers are warm but not oppressive, and the grapes here mature slowly and calmly." He crouched down in the soil. "These vines are kept at a certain height above the ground so they can receive more sunlight and be protected from the frosts." He brushed his hands over the bottoms of the vines with care. He'd removed his blazer and rolled up the sleeves of his white shirt. All of a sudden, the trip was not intimidating. The information, coming from Heinrich, was not loaded with any history or expectation. It was clean.

"You see, wine defies objective material description. It is a tool for conviviality, a bond between people, and is therefore totally subjective. The bond is reflected in the vines—an earth-and-sky bond."

I turned to my dad and elbowed him gently in the ribs. He looked happy.

"Alors, on va aller voire la récolte." Heinrich wanted to show us the day's harvest and thrust his chin in the direction of a set of stone stairs. They led up to a second and third tier of vines. Above them was the swanky hotel Château Isenbourg and the mammoth processing area where the grapes were having their current lives squeezed out of them.

For all the talk of the careful hand plucking of the grapes, and the vines' dual link to the heavens and the soil and all things earthly and human and spiritual, I was surprised as hell to see that the bulk of the work was being done by robots. Massive, whirring, crushing robots. The air was jammed with mechanized noises and organic noises; for every *bjjjjj-zzzzzeeeoooo* and *pffsshhhhhhhh* there were a thousand long, wet squishes. It was thrilling, this breathless preservation and transmutation of the harvest.

"Robots!" My voice was a ripple. I was entranced.

The rickety pickup trucks were in the overhead unloading zone, dumping their luscious bounty into a wild, screwy rotating machine that blitzed away stems and leaves, creating overflowing piles of clean little scrotums that were pushed dripping and languid into massive cylindrical containers the size of two and a half full-grown African elephants, then squashed slowly, chokingly, by the round pneumatic squashers. One vat was full of Gewurztraminer, another full of Pinot Noir. Forming my four fingers into a small cup, I let them run under the tiny dripping silver taps sticking out of the presses. The juice was still warm, the grape skins having served as an incubator to retain the heat from the sun in the fields. It tasted fresh, clean, ambrosially sweet.

"*C'est bon, hein?*" Heinrich came upon me as I was sucking on my index finger with spasmodic relish.

"*Oh, monsieur, excusez-moi.*" I wiped my hands along the length of my hips and thighs.

"*Non, non . . . Ça va. C'est absolument délicieux, ce jus!*"

I finished fellating my finger and nodded in agreement . . . it was *absolument délicieux*. I wanted to position my face underneath the taps and suck dry this mighty teat.

We clunked and clanged up an industrial metal staircase for a bird's-eye view of the tanks. The Pinot Noir container was wearing a thick hat of its deflated grape skins. Over the sounds of the machines, I yelled at my father for a translation.

"Dad, what's the grape skin hat called?"

"The pomace," he shouted back.

"Right. Good. And the whole thing—the new pressings and all—is the must, huh?"

"The must, yes."

"And so the hat gives it character. The character depends on how long the hat is left on."

"Yes. Like men." He grinned.

"Like a man wearing a hat," I confirmed.

One by one, the trucks—their outsides spattered with brown muck and their insides stained with inky juice—fired up and cruised away into an early evening as ridiculously vivid as a fistful of sunflower petals. We reached out for another round of handshakes with Heinrich and Jumpy Man. Heinrich reiterated his earlier invitation to have us meet with Pfaffenheim's head sommelier for a wine tasting in the morning. As they turned and walked off, I crammed the tips of the fingers of my right hand into my mouth and scraped my bottom teeth along my nails, dislodging the remaining bits of teat juice. Out of nowhere my father's arm appeared, slapping my hand away from my probing tongue.

"You are disgus*teeng*," he said. Then he cackled.

At the Château Isenbourg, I was in my room taking mental notes on the hotel wallpaper: a Toile de Jouy depicting a kind of elephant safari, with colonialist women riding on elephants, some in profile, some in portrait, palm trees with elephants standing near them and rocks with elephants standing on top. It was silly wallpaper, really. I felt safe and solid, and I wanted to make a joke about this dumb elephant wallpaper. But not with my father. I wanted to make a joke with Matthew. I wanted to tell him about how poorly the trip had been going and about the triumph of today. I wanted to hear how his days had been and whether he'd been missing me. So I located our international cell phone and sent him a text message. I shooed away the creeping voices. *You're torturing him by doing this. Let him alone.*

Staring at the small gray screen of the phone, I waited for an answer, even though it was early over there, too early to be replying to text messages from ex-girlfriends. Matthew was an insomniac. There was a chance.

I punched a trough into the unused feather pillow lying to my right and nestled the phone into the dent. I drifted off, and the phone didn't beep.

chapter eight

Early daylight seeped into my room, causing me to flop over impatiently onto my stomach and force my head between the crevasse of the two stacks of pillows. My left arm immediately touched cold plastic. I regained a bit of consciousness. *The phone.* I slid it around in my hand until the screen was upright, then brought it in close to my face with dread and hope.

What would the message say?

What would it say!

He'd always responded. Matthew was my first responder. During one of our sleepovers (always at my apartment, never his), he'd been waiting for me to finish brushing my teeth. The door was closed, as I'd made it clear that new lovers should not watch each other perform any bathroom-specific duties of grooming and function. Patiently, he'd waited outside the door to brush his own teeth. My cheap electric toothbrush—one that ran on AA batteries—buzzed weakly each time I applied its head to my teeth. I grumbled swear words and rapped the thing on the counter. Matthew asked if I was okay. I said I was okay and grumbled some more, eventually emerging after having given up on the magic electric life force of the toothbrush. I'd worn out the bristles with a vigorous manual brushing and chucked it in the garbage.

The next day, we were standing in the lunch line of a Thai restaurant in a food court. Tapping me on the shoulder, he said, "I have a small surprise for you," and made me reach into the kangaroo pocket of his zip-up sweatshirt. Inside was a new toothbrush.

Whenever I made it clear in sentences and in movements and in grumbles that I required the Body and Brain of My Boyfriend, he stretched out those branch-arms of his and I was immediately encircled. He was my safety. My eyes remained closed.

He is not yours anymore.

I knew there would be no message from him.

When I ended my relationship with him, I did it all wrong. Really, there are only two ways of breaking up with a person. Option 1: Selfishly. Option 2: Unselfishly. Unselfishly is the correct option and feels awful, as it should. To be the person who has already surreptitiously removed their heart from the table and to then discontinue a partnership with a person whose heart remains on the table all gooey and throbbing and exposed relegates the discontinuer to doing one and only one job.

That job is to eat shit with a shovel. Great piles of shit, loaded up onto a gleaming shovel.

If I'd been correct, unselfish, I would have stormed in quickly, pressed my C-4 plastic explosives into the crags and gaps, set off the detonator, and run like hell. I would not have stuck around for post-attack negotiations, or for rebuilding efforts, or to play soccer with my orphan who'd just lost his hand and part of his rib cage; I would have gotten in and gotten out. Zoom. And after walking farther and farther away from the disaster zone, only *then* would I have been allowed to ask myself questions. I would have been able to analyze how I'd been cruel and if I was all broken and split like old gray driftwood. I would have been permitted to ask if the union was not love but some twisted vanity project to temporarily sate a much larger, more intricate hunger. Only *then* could I have pondered and doubted my capability to discriminate between Cupid's golden arrow and his lead arrow, wines of meditation and wines that required no real investment or concentration.

If I'd been good, I would have done all this questioning far away from him, in my room or quietly on my short, depressed jogs. Only *there* would I have been allowed to describe myself as "an emotional slut" who was "dead inside," like an ancient, hollowed-out gourd with a sad little pile of dried-up seeds amassed at the bottom that made an even sadder plinking sound when I walked.

There, alone, I would have had license to do this kind of thinking while trying to silence the plinking noises by forcing piles of crispy bacon and cream-based pasta sauces into my mouth and far too much thick, microbrewed beer down my throat. If I'd been considerate of him, I would have allowed myself to go blobby so that when I was faced with seeing him at work, he would be in the luxurious position of gushing to his friends that I'd become fat, jiggly, and altogether unlovable—and furthermore undatable—since the breakup. Of course he'd never say that, but I should have become overweight to give him the opportunity. Or I should have at least *wanted* to give him the opportunity.

But I didn't.

I had *not* smiled resolutely as I watched previously bipartisan friends choose a side that was not mine and did not focus on my shoelaces when I ran into them in the street, knowing them to be judging what I'd done based on the intelligence they were obtaining solely from Matthew. Instead, I'd trap them and batter them with a babbling stream of excuses, justifications, corrections. I did not stoically read one friend's biting e-mail and did not sob in agreement over her refusal to be sympathetic to my plight, her incapacity for stroking me between the eyes. She said I should have known better than to lead him on when I did not want him (had I ever truly wanted him? she'd asked. *OF COURSE*, I'd screamed angrily to myself, at my computer screen). She was *not* right, I *could* continue to use the line "Oh, poor me, I'm so fucked up!" as an excuse for vain behavior. That was my *birthright*. It was absolutely appropriate that I cast myself in the starring role of this drama. He was in pain, but *I too* was in pain. And no, it was *not* time I grew up. I was still but a girl!

But if I'd been unselfish, I would have just accepted all the brokenness, all the thoughtless cruelty. I would have studied my vanity and my proclivity for love odds that ruled in my favor. The cowardly tendency for unilateral adulation.

And if I'd been smarter, I would have sat in my emotional bunker eating canned pears (and shoveled shit and bacon and pasta), waiting for the air to clear so that out of it, I could pluck some truth to apply to the next man. To myself. *That* would have been the correct course of action.

With Matthew, I chose to be selfish.

We worked so well in a foxhole. We cooked together. He was good at knowing how much salt I liked in my food. When one of us would get quiet and sad, the other would walk up, stick out a finger, and press it into a piece of flesh. Then we'd say, "Poke." The worse it seemed, the softer and closer to the face the pokes would become. If it was really bad, it would be just the slightest poke on the cheek, with the most hushed and whispery, "*Poke.*"

His commitment to me was doubtless, unflinching. He calmly abided my rants and extremes, my constant hunger and dissatisfaction with myself, with life, with everything. During our first February together, on the weekend before the twenty-third, I'd attended a party where I knew barely anybody. The people were older, the friend I'd come with left early. I'd been talking to a gaunt woman. As she became drunker, she detailed her recent back surgery and offered me some of her pain medication. I gobbled down the pill and asked for another, for later. She gave me two.

When I called Matthew's apartment at five in the morning from a taxi, my voice falsetto with panic, a swamp for a head, having forgotten where I was and where I lived, he patiently fed me words to relay to the cabdriver. When I pulled up in front of my house, Matthew was there, in the cold with no jacket on, waiting on my front steps, his boots unlaced, his cell phone in his bare hand.

"I brought your spare key, just in case," he said.

I described to him my allergy to the present. Matthew nodded patiently when I stomped around, detailing how I could not exist within or enjoy the present (even though he was in mine) and how it had pressurizing and irritating effects on the contents of my skull (which, at the time, included him). He abided this allergy—at once an itch and a fear. An itch that could be scratched only by getting on with it, moving on to the next thing, satisfying the curiosity that there is something beyond *this* place, this annoying purgatory that is holding up my trajectory to the *other* place—the other place, of course, being much better and more stimulating than *this* infernal place. He internalized how my itch paled in comparison with my fear. The fear of *this* place ending. The fear that this place was, in fact, the best place, and it was moments away from ending. The fear that I would not be in this place again, that once it was gone all the feelings would also be gone, and not gone momentarily, but gone forever.

He got how the itch, at least, was an enabler, whereas the fear, contrarily, precluded my happiness and made me wonder why I bothered doing anything at all. And he didn't seem afraid of any of it. He didn't seem terrified. Not even at the beginning, not even during our first beer date at a greasy Toronto Tex-Mex restaurant, when I was acting itchy, so itchy, and I stared at him like a creep in his striped long-sleeved shirt with its flattering collar that emphasized his smooth, boyish neck. I sat there pouring pitchers of beer into our glasses. I encouraged him to drink faster and faster. We became drunk, and he smiled an amused smile when I thrashed my arms at the waitress as though I were an epileptic air traffic controller, demanding she bring us our bill and four shots of repulsive German liqueur so that I could drown out the faint final voice in my head's Greek chorus that was meekly crying, *Don't kiss him in the restaurant, it's tacky and you have nacho breath.* And he didn't mind when I scooted off my bench, pivoted across the width of the table, plunked down next to him, and thrust my face into his.

Weeks later I announced, "We're a couple now!"

He replied, "Sure. I wasn't planning on going anywhere."

He was never heartless, the way Peter had been during those brutal months after the accident, when I was still consumed with depression, when he yelled, "If your knee is broken, you go see a knee doctor. If your head is broken, you go see a head doctor." If Matthew made a Face of Intense Contemplation, and I asked him what he was thinking, he would not say something like "Oh, nothing . . ." or "I don't feel like talking about it; I am a very private person, you know." He would just come out with it and allow me to help him, if I could. A lot of the time I couldn't, because he didn't believe the things I told him about himself. But most of the time, when we were alone in the little quiet egg of our love, at least he let me try.

When I had a bad day at work, he'd take me out for coffee and quietly sing Lyle Lovett's "If I Had a Boat." He'd look straight ahead and sing the opening until I was hysterical with laughter:

"If I had a boat / I'd go out on the ocean / And if I had a pony / I'd ride him on my boat / And we could all to-gether / Go out on the ocean / Just me upon my pony on my boat."

When I broke up with him, he stayed with me, in my house. He stayed because I had just been walloped with a bout of stomach flu, and despite his broken heart he stayed with me for three days, feeding me Jell-O and applesauce. He stayed also because I was not brave. I was selfish and turned into a huge sobbing mass of muscle and flesh and blood and whimpered that I loved him and would always, always love him and how I couldn't imagine a world without him and his collection of different-colored polo shirts.

As he spoon-fed me applesauce through my tears, he said, "I'm not sure I understand what you're telling me."

To which I should have responded, "I'm breaking up with you, now you must leave. Thank you for the applesauce, but I can feed it to myself."

To which I instead responded, "I love you and want you in my life, but I can't appropriate your existential dread anymore."

To which he responded, "Does this mean we're breaking up?"

To which I responded, "Yes."

Then added, "I still love you."

My weakness set us on course for three months of beige. I wrote the rules with his tacit consent. We could spend as much time as we wanted together. Phone calls were unlimited. Physical contact was discouraged, but permitted when we lazily or drunkenly blundered into it, as long as it was completely dry. A head on a lap during a rented movie, fine. Sleepovers were okay, as long as we were fully clothed and our bodies were shaped in the form of spoons. We did not speak of romantic rendezvous with other humans, especially me, who in my beige freedom had taken to engaging in romantic rendezvousing with three other men. My life took on the dual shape of a juggling act and a sexy Venn diagram. And in the week before my departure for France, I had a hunch that Matthew—who tap-danced between the territories of supreme perceptiveness and outright paranoia—began putting the pieces together.

In my hotel room, I'd fallen back into a fitful sleep under the Toile de Jouy elephant wallpaper. I was skateboarding around an asbestos pit to avoid a group of zombies who seemed intent on acquiring my brain or spraying infected zombie blood all over my face. I couldn't make out whether they were the slow, atrophied late-twentieth-century zombies or the fast, rabid early-twenty-first-century zombies. *Is it a group of zombies? A pack of zombies? A herd of zombies?* Whatever it was, I was terrified and skating fast, planting my foot firmly into the gravelly earth, swooping down the arc of the pit, throwing my weight forward as I hit the upward slant, all the while looking back, checking to see how much terrain I'd gained on the zombies. There was Kate Moss in the middle of the pit, sitting on a splintery wooden bench. She was all in white. What was she doing here, in this pit? The cuffs of her white jeans were absorbing the gray brown dirt like denim sponges. The zombies had no interest in her. Oh, she was kissing Matthew. Matthew and Kate Moss, me and the zombies. Curious. There was pounding. Pounding, a fist on wood; someone was at the door. *What door?* Rap rap rap. Room service. *Room service can't help me now. Room service?*

"ROOM SERVICE!"

Dad. Outside.

Fuck. Matthew. He knows. He knows I used him. But he might not know. How would he know? Did I use him? Would it be easier if he thought I didn't really love him, and that was it?

I saw him on my front steps, shivering in the cold, hearing his voice through my cell phone but also in my other ear. I'd never even asked for the spare key to his apartment. I couldn't have given him that safety.

"Room *SERVEEEECE.*"

My eyes were heavy and sticky from dreaming too hard.

I jammed my thumb and index finger parallel to my ocular cavities and wrenched up the lids, blinking and blinking. In my openmouthed dream stupor, each of my teeth had been covered with a little woolly sock. Feeling like 152 bucks and a bit chubby, I rolled over to the pillow trough and checked the phone once more, to be sure. No envelope icon. No movement. No nothing. *He knows. He must know.* My colon became a knot of dread. I should have been brave. And honest. I was now too far away to mitigate the hurt, the damage. *I am treacherous.*

"ROOM *Serveeeeeeeece.*"

I envied this man's ability to endure—no, be infinitely enchanted—by his own jokes. Room service. *Yes, Dad, you are room service, which is why you are at my door, knocking and knocking, just as a room service attendant does.*

Answering the door, I found my father standing in the middle of the hallway. A couple of chic Europeans with leather luggage sets flattened themselves against the wall to get by, carefully maneuvering their belongings to avoid touching him. His outfit was a pair of untied sneakers and a set of dripping navy swim trunks. They were a touch too short. He reeked of chlorine and was not wearing a shirt; his chest rug was wet and matted.

"Hello, would you like some room *serveeeece?*" He was grinning broadly.

"You swam?"

"I went to the spa. I ran in the water. It is something I learned to do in Kenya."

"You did Aquabics in Kenya?"

"It's low impact. Good for my knees."

"Old people do Aquabics."

"I am not old."

"You are old."

"You're right, I am old."

"Obviously, because you do Aquabics. Come into the room. People are staring. Your hair looks like the hair of a freshly hatched baby chicken."

He flopped down on the heavy woven bedspread, snatched my paddle hairbrush, and gave his scalp a once-over.

"Kissum." He pointed his cheek up to me. I gave him *la bise*.

"Enough!" he said.

I grabbed the brush back from him, then performed a slow tap dance away from the bed, over to the mirror.

"Did you dream?" My father is one of three people I know who is interested in hearing others' dreams.

"I did. Mainly right before I woke up. One of those dreams that lasts a thousand years and leaves you feeling more exhausted than you did before you went to bed. You know? I was being chased by zombies. In a pit. I was on a skateboard."

"Ah. This probably means you were not hugged enough as a child."

"You're probably right."

"Do you want to hear mine?"

"Bring it on, turkey."

"I was having group sex."

There was no section in the *Father-Daughter User Manual* for these circumstances.

I waited a beat. "Hm. Was Blondie there, at least?"

"No. But there was a shark. I was having group sex, and I was getting the most attention from a shark. I thought to myself, *This aaaiiin't good,* and then I woke up."

"This probably means you weren't hugged enough as a child."

"Heheh. Precisely."

He paused and studied my face. "You look tired, sweet thing."

"Mm. Yeah. Right. I texted Matthew last night and he didn't respond."

"So? He maybe didn't receive the message yet. Or he's busy."

"Maybe. I'm just in a bit of a paranoid place. I was a little, oh, what's the word, like, eh, overzealous after I broke up with Matthew."

"Overzealous how?"

This is the part where I admit to my father that I am a slut. A few years ago, the two of us went fishing for a day. We spent most of the day coming up with NHL offensive strategies for catching trout and screaming, *"Go away, grass!"* when our hooks would dredge up the slimy phytochemical sludge at the bottom of the lake. Between these two activities, we managed to share a handful of bonding moments—one of which was him admitting to me that he had been a lothario before his marriage to Bernadette, his first wife, and during one of their separations, a decade before he met my mother. I asked him how many women he had bedded, and he said, *"Environ soixante."* About sixty. Since then, I'd been toiling diligently to surpass him. For a while, I was trying to work my way through the alphabet. But Q's, U's, X's, Y's, and Z's are almost impossible to find.

"Overzealous in that I've become involved with three men. I mean, boys. They're not that old. Dudes. You know, dudes," I stuttered. "But it's more complicated than that—"

"We will call them the Three Tenors," he interrupted. He was joking, but curious. This was the first time we'd spoken of my sex life. My father's eyes darted around the room. I couldn't tell what he was thinking.

"Sure, okay. The Three Tenors. Fine." I wanted to tell him the rest, to say, "But there's other stuff, Dad. It's more complicated than the Three Tenors. My feelings are broken. And I wonder if they're broken because of you."

"And so?"

I sighed and went on. "And so Matthew is sharp, and has a tendency to be catastrophic . . ."

"Like you."

"Like me, yes, right. Anyway, he's a catastrophizer—and I'm concerned he might know that I've been dating."

"Dating the Three Tenors."

"Yes. Dating the Three Tenors."

"Sleeping with them all?"

"Yes. All of them."

"But you are no longer together, with Matthew."

"No."

"But you are friends."

"Yeah, but there are boundaries in these situations. Full transparency can be hurtful. I don't want to hurt him."

"Then why do you still speak with him?"

"Because . . . because I still care about him."

"An ex-lover cannot be the one who comforts an ex-lover," he said sternly.

"I know."

"It's unethical."

"I know it is."

"Tootsie, you have to be fair to people. It is a potent blend, what you've been given. Genetics have been your friend. You have your mother's sensitivity and my charisma. That can be deadly to a gentle soul. Right?"

"Right. Right? I don't know. Thank you. For the compliment. Let's go. I am hungry for food."

Outside, it was a gusty morning, and the first weak leaves were quivering off the trees like golden Post-it notes.

"Go left." My father was settling into his role as navigator.

"Dad, my only option is to go left."

I was not focusing well, caught between a cross-fade of paranoia: all the latent meaning contained within the failure of my relationship with Matthew . . . and today's wine tasting. But the cross-fade became caught in the middle. *But there is also latent meaning in wine.* My paranoia doubled as I dragged all the Matthew luggage into what was supposed to be a pleasant midmorning activity. My pastry breakfast sat like lead in my stomach.

I needed a tinfoil helmet and an Ativan.

"Tootsie?" My father was watching me.

"Hello," I said.

"Are you tense?"

"Ehm . . . yes."

"Can I help?"

"Ehm . . . no?"

"No?"

"I don't think so."

"Are you nervous about the tasting?"

"Yes."

"Why are you nervous?"

"Why do you think I'm nervous? I am afraid of another disaster. I am afraid of looking like a *jackass*," I said. The words were too forceful, imbalanced.

"But you are not a jackass."

"I just feel like I'm going to say all the wrong things. Like I'll describe the wines incorrectly."

"But there is nothing wrong to say, there is no 'incorrect,' if what you're saying is the honest impression of what you are tasting."

"Oh, come on. It's not that easy."

"It is."

"It's not."

"It is, really."

After pulling into the lot, I parked the car exactly between two spots; the white spray-painted line stretched out beneath the car, dividing it in two perfectly.

Inside the Pfaffenheim headquarters, on the ground floor, there was a beautiful, silent wineshop. At the back, a dark wooden bar stretched out, the wall behind it top-lit with soft yellow bulbs that showcased neat lineups of the winery's bottles. The floor was gleaming, the sunlight fizzing through an opaque layer of clouds and through the windows, giving all objects and persons an angelic tinge. Someone had set up a large round table for our visit, covered it in a carefully ironed white tablecloth, and dressed the tablecloth with a square arrangement of four wineglasses and an elegant black spittoon resembling a mod version of a Rubens vase. Aesthetically, we could not be further from Rémy's mushroomy cellar and all my old memories of my father's New Jersey cave. For this, I was grateful. The place looked like a hotel. The wines were always put in storage when we lived in hotels.

We stood in waiting. My dad scanned through his Day-Timer—his *bréviaire*—shuffling pages. The room smelled a bit antiseptic. I pressed my tongue to the roof of my mouth, moving it back and forth so the taste buds would become warm with spit and friction, stopping when I realized that my tongue was not my quadriceps and this was not Race Day at school.

"What happens next?" I asked.

A man behind the bar, who up until that point had been blending seamlessly into the ecosystem, raised his hand as if answering a question. He was wearing a white starched shirt, a black scoop-necked apron, and a bow tie. If he'd removed the apron and outfitted himself with a pocket protector, he would have looked like a professor of mathematics at the University of Munich. He was friendly and nebbishy and precise-looking, his face an oval, tidy brown hair.

"Bonjour."

"Bernard Nast?" my father said.

"Bernard Nast."

I did a quick inventory of questions I would avoid asking. *No questions about soil, none about the north, south, east, or westerly directions of the vines and what impact this might have on the grapes. No technical questions, nothing about the types of pneumatic presses the winery uses to extract the juice.*

Bernard Nast and my father were in the middle of the getting-to-know-you back-and-forth. Blah blah blah, she's a journalist, I'm with Fairmont, blah blah blah.

I would not ask about aging, what kinds of barrels were used. Whether I knew the wine sat in French or American oak barrels was irrelevant for now. Maybe on another trip, maybe one through another country, like Italy or Argentina, I would be accomplished enough to glean why certain varietals need very hot days and cool nights in order to develop properly.

Nast was collecting bottles, placing them two by two in the middle of the immaculate tablecloth. He and my father were still chatting; they had moved on to the subject of Robert Parker, the famed wine critic whom my father was describing as *"un homme constipé."* Parker is one of the most influential voices on wine in the world and, many years ago, developed a 1–100 rating system for wines, which was perplexing, based on what my father had told me in the car and what Alex Heinrich had said in his vineyard. If I were to believe these men, objectively defining any sensual pleasure would be akin to developing a rating system for, say, making love. *If a man dressed up in a giant periwinkle bunny costume before bedding me, I would likely rate that experience a 2 out of 100, with 10 or 15 points of available added value depending on his technical aptitude. But if I were a furvert, the rating would surely be much higher.* According to my father, Parker was the same. *The only difference is the man in the plushie outfit is an expansively flavored, easy-seducing wine with little nuance.*

Okay! A passable simile! Focus on wine and words. That is the game plan. Wine, I know how to drink. I put it in my mouth, I let air run through my mouth, I swallow, and I say some words that are honest and true to the experience. Simple. Easy. Consume and speak. These are my second and third favorite pastimes!

Two small oblong wicker baskets full of fresh baguette, cut into cubes, bracketed the group of green bottles huddled on the tabletop. In total, there were thirteen. *Lucky thirteen. Lucky me. Really, though, lucky me.* I was flummoxed by Nast's generosity—these were not cheap castoffs; there must have been five hundred dollars' worth of wine sitting there quietly, like little musical theater actors waiting to tap-dance onto the scene and sing us the show tune they'd prepared.

"Asseyez-vous, s'il vous plaît," Nast said.

He waved us into the plush banquette surrounding the table and uncorked one of the tap dancers. My father flipped open his Day-Timer, adjusted his glasses, and wrote down the label details.

Rooting around in my satchel, I searched for writing implements. *God, have I brought any?* At the airport in Montreal, I had scanned the meager collection of notebooks at the French bookstore, and all had gay children's motifs—juggling cartoon bears or mice wearing bonnets, doing anachronistic human activities, riding penny-farthing bicycles or churning butter. Crap like that. My hand touched a leatherlike material. *Excellent.* I'd brought my small desk calendar—a compact red book bound in what looked to be fake alligator skin, yes, the wily red fake alligator of south-central Peru. This would do fine. I had no pen, so I steadied my M•A•C lip pencil in my left hand, hoping my father and Nast would not notice. I tested the solidity of the tip. It smeared all over the place. Adjusting my hand, I hovered the pencil farther away from the page and tried writing again. *Why didn't you bring a PEN? There were PENS all over the hotel room. PENS. How are you supposed to focus on LANGUAGE and FEELINGS when you don't even have a proper PEN?*

Nast served two inches of four different wines and placed the bottles in front of our glasses, labels out, in sequence. I copied the label haltingly. Clos Château Isenbourg, 2002, Pinot Blanc. Château Isenbourg, the name of our hotel, the hotel that used to be an actual château. I nervously circled "Clos." The translation was escaping me. *Clos clos clos-clos/cos . . .*

Clos. Closed. Enclosure. The château had been surrounded by a short stone enclosure. A tiny victory. I bucked up a little.

The second was a blend of Pinot Blanc, Riesling, and Tokay Pinot Gris. Les Tourelles, 2004. Then another Les Tourelles, but exclusively Riesling, 2002. And a Pfaffenheim Grand Cru Steinert, 2001.

I slid my index and middle fingers around the stem of the first glass, rested my hand over its thin base, and swirled confidently and smoothly, so the light golden liquid shimmied up the sides of the glass in swelling waves. I pinched the stem in my claw, brought the glass to my face, and shoved my nose in deep, way beyond the rim, as if I were a junkie huffing turpentine. I sipped, drew in a little air, and rippled my tongue against my upper palate to let the air circulate, then swallowed. Nast was doing the same, as was my dad. We set down our wineglasses. My moves were accomplished. These were moves I'd learned from my father. I relaxed and waited for the words to come.

My father's eyes were fixed on my face. I averted them and looked at Nast. Nast was staring at my father. I looked back at my father, who was now staring at the bottom of the glass. Air rumbled in my trachea as I gargled some nonformed words. When I opened my mouth to breathe, the sound came out like a low, dying animal groan. *Not yet, not yet.* Nast stared at me; I tightened the corners of my mouth into an awkward metal grin and stared back into the wine in my own glass.

My father took another sip and took a note. Squinting slightly, hopefully inconspicuously, I cast my eyes sideways toward the writing. Illegible. His writing was always crushed and dramatically horizontal, easy to forge, impossible to read. Finally, Nast opened his mouth to speak.

"January was cold, in 2002," he said.

I nodded knowingly. *Yes, a cold January. Cold Januaries are cold. January is one of the top three months people choose to commit suicide. That is a fun fact I know about January.* How a cold January affected grapes, I did not know. *Aren't grapes picked by January?* I lightly pressed the lip pencil onto the lines of my desk calendar to mark "cold January, 2002" under a gray circle that told me that on June 10, I'd apparently had a meeting with my friend Stuart Berman. The fatty plum wax gooped onto the page again and smudged as my hand dragged over the writing. This was insane. I needed a real pen.

"Monsieur Nast, could I trouble you for a pen or pencil?"

He reached into his shirt pocket, smiled, and fished one out. My dad knocked my leg under the table. I couldn't tell if it was playful or disdainful.

"The spring was rainy, but what salvaged the grapes was a big heat from August to September."

I scribbled away. We tasted the next wine, Nast gave a précis of what the circumstances were, and then we tasted the next. At the fourth, my father was moved to comment.

"Mm," he said.

I took a desperate sip, fervent to follow along. "Mm," I mimicked.

OH, RELAX.

Loosening my shoulders, I took in a deep breath. Then something happened. The wine, which had disappeared down my throat, reappeared in fragrance. But it was bigger than the initial flavor. It was *huge.*

I took another sip, swallowed, and it performed the same trick.

"Oh. Mmmm!"

"T'aime ça, Kathryn?" Nast said.

"Oui! C'est . . . uh . . . long." *It's long in the mouth. It sticks around. It's getting in one last good flirt with my tongue before it disappears, turning around at all angles so I can check it out.*

"That's one of its qualities—it has a presence, this wine," Nast said.

"Yes. Presence, yes!" I nearly shouted.

"Belle étoffe," my father said.

"What's *étoffe*?" I asked.

"Material. Silky material," he answered.

"Yeah, like there's a tiny, fancy housekeeper and she's putting a sheet on a bed by snapping it up and down, letting it billow around the mattress. It's like that pocket of air underneath the billow," I marveled.

"Heh. Not a bad image, Tootsen."

I beamed, he beamed. The last time I saw him beam like this was when I volunteered to make a hollandaise sauce for asparagus he was steaming for dinner. He said, "When I was a cook you had to wait years to be allowed to prepare the hollandaise." I said, "Dad, trust me." I shoved a wrapped stick of butter in my back pocket, walked around the house for a few minutes, then whisked a bowlful of textbook hollandaise. He fell silent with pride and told me I was amazing.

"What's the grape?"

My father dragged the bottle close. "Pinot Blanc," he said.

"Fresh," I said.

"Viny," he said.

Nast poured a round of 1999 Tokay Pinot Gris. We tasted.

"Elegant," I said.

"Yes. But authoritarian."

"An iron fist in a velvet glove?" I hazarded, too quickly.

"Maybe. But you are better than these clichés, Tootsen," he said.

"I'm trying," I said.

"I know." He put his hand over mine.

We tasted a battalion of 2003s from the clos, a Pinot Gris, a Riesling, and a Gewurztraminer.

"These are babies," my father said.

"Charming babies," I said. He nodded and took a note. "Charming babies you don't even want to kick across a room." At this, my dad cackled.

A clearer light flooded through the window, turning the

white of the tablecloth silvery and marking my father's and Nast's foreheads with a glowing square. I was a little drunk and extremely happy. Or extremely drunk and a little happy. Probably the former, and full of crusty bread cubes. Either way, my throat kept catching when I breathed in, an audible flutter of relief and joy.

Nast uncorked the final bottle, a 1999 Gewurztraminer Grains Nobles. It was a dessert wine, pale gold, velvety, and sweet.

"We do wine workshops with children here," Nast said as he distributed the honeyed stuff.

"The children drink?" I asked. *Ah, France.*

"Yes, we give them a taste at the end of the tour. We show them the vineyards, the machines. Mr. Heinrich talks to them. They draw pictures, and then we give them little glasses of sweet wine."

"I find children far more agreeable to be around when they are drunk. And I am drunk," I said.

The men said nothing.

"Monsieur Nast, 'Grains Nobles' refers to grapes that have been affected by botrytis fungus, right?"

"Exactly."

"The noble rot," I confirmed.

"Oui. La pourriture noble," he reconfirmed.

If there were a feature-length article on the noble rot in a tabloid magazine, the title would read, "Bad Rot Makes Good." I remembered being at home on a long weekend years ago and finding a wine manual—the 1987–1988 Sommelier Executive Council's *Vintage Wine Book*. It was ugly and blue and appeared to have been put together by teenage workers at Kinko's. Before I left, I stole it off my parents' bookshelf, thinking that I would study it for an hour every day until I came home again and blow my dad's mind during our next tasting. It was a short-lived attempt—Peter and I broke up a few weeks later and I cast aside the project. Given the circumstances, I *had* retained one fact—the difference between shitty normal rot and the noble rot.

The noble rot is the Midas touch for certain sweet wines. The process is magical, as the shit kind of the rot and the good kind of the rot come from the same fungus, *Botrytis cinerea*. This fungus is gray and filmy and forms when the weather is a special certain type of wet. If the weather remains wet, and the gray rot forms and sticks around, the grapes are, as the French say, *foutu* (fucked). The grapes become deflated, stanky, and unusable. But! If the moist weather is followed by a dry spell, the fungus begins wasting away the grape, sucking out its water content, and turning it into a more raisinlike berry.

These berries are picked, sometimes one by one, crushed, and used to make sumptuously concentrated sweet wines: Sauternes in the Bordeaux region, Tokaji in Hungary, Beerenauslese and Trockenbeerenauslese in Austria and Germany, and Grains Nobles here in Alsace.

Maybe you are not riddled with shitty rot after all. Maybe your confusion about Matthew, about men, is like that initial rot—it can go either way.

We thanked Nast for the tasting, and thanked him again when he hurried back and forth across the store to make us a gift of three bottles of Pfaffenheim wines.

"Merci *beaucoup*." I leaned in to give Nast the *bise*. He returned mine. We waved at him through the car window, and I did two little blasts on the horn. *Yip yip.*

"You were very charming today, Tootsen. Very charming, very smart. Nast liked you very much, it was clear." My father was looking straight ahead, down the road that would lead us to Burgundy.

"Thank you," I said. There was helium in my chest.

"And this evening, we will arrive in the land of Pinot Noir. You are a—"

"A Burgundy. I know, you said that before. Why? What do you mean?"

"You will see, I think, when we get there."

The narrow road became highway. I sped up.

chapter nine

"You obviously had an early penchant for wine, Tootsie. You became drunk six months after you were born, at Christmastime."

We were speeding south. My father was telling me my story. His story. All the stories. My heart was full to the brim. Occasionally, when I pour water into a cup, I'll look away and fixate on a thought or an item in the room. Then I will hear splashing, look down, and realize I've poured water in the cup, filled it, and the water has begun to trickle down the edge of the counter like a tiny waterfall and is splashing onto the floor. Now it was my father's turn to do this, but my heart was the cup. For now, we had found our language.

He paused. "What year were you born in?" He is excellent at history, can rattle off the birth dates of most of the bottles in his cellar, but not the vintages of his children. Occasionally, I'll quiz him about my birthday. "June twentieth?" There is always a question mark at the end of his answers. "June twenty-third, Dad. You're getting closer." He used to think it was June 17.

He explained that I was introduced to the concept of wine in our twelfth-floor converted apartment at the Loews Westbury Hotel in Toronto, where he was the manager. The apartment had seen many sparkling people. Celebrity guests at the hotel would be invited up to our place for elegant cocktail parties. They would use our eternal supply of small, aggressively floral-smelling soaps and our fresh toilet rolls—always fat and fluffy, never sad and shredded—with the last square folded and tucked into a downward-pointing arrow. We have snapshots in old family albums—my father standing next to heavyweight boxer Smokin' Joe Frazier, captured in grainy black and white, Frazier smiling on the balcony, squinting in the sun, my father, visibly stirred, stealing an emotional glance at him. A photo of Björn Borg—who won Wimbledon five times and the French Open six—his curly bangs tucked under a terry-cloth headband, positioned behind my mother, awkward but ecstatic in her tennis whites, Björn teaching her how to correctly swing through a backhand. One of me, a pudgy, squishy, tomato-faced infant in the arms of the incendiary U.S. Open champion Ilie Năstase.

"He thought you were cute, Ilie Năstase," Dad said, "but

remember, this is also the same man who showed up to play a match against Arthur Ashe in blackface."

"What are you saying?"

"That you were a *vahree* ugly baby. You looked like a cross between a pit bull and Winston Churchill," he said.

"Thanks."

He reached out, tweaked my earlobe, and continued.

Apparently, on the day of my accidental alcoholic indoctrination, my parents were entertaining a distinctly less illustrious crowd. It was December 23, and the Borels were having a family Christmas party for the Blackmores, my mother's side of the family. All British, the Blackmores had not yet wholly embraced my father's presence in their clan.

"They were wary of me," said my father. "I am French. They found me bizarre. They did not feel comfortable with the ten-year age difference between Blondie and me, maybe. And of course, we were not yet married. Your grandfather called me his 'sin-in-law.'"

I snorted and drummed my hands on the steering wheel. A bug exploded on the windshield.

Given the context, the evening called for dramatic amounts of booze, so my dad ordered many bottles of wine, enough to fell a battalion of Charles Bukowskis. As the evening wore on and the bottles were drained, I was left to cruise around the living room with the help of my Exer-Saucer, a streamlined contraption made of plastic and vinyl that looks not unlike a cross between a harness, a lounge chair, and a small spaceship on wheels—for babies who have not yet mastered the art of bipedalism. I might not have known how to walk, but I definitely knew how to maneuver the ExerSaucer, and I absolutely knew how to drink; and because no one in the room could tolerate one another if they were drinking water, all that was available for drinking on those low-lying 1970s-style tables were the red and white alcoholic dregs at the bottoms of various glasses.

"And that is what you drank," my father said.

"Did you take me to the hospital?"

"No. Blondie found you in a pile in your little machine. You were crying a little bit. When she removed you, you began screaming and being sick."

"Funny."

Funny. A harbinger of what was to come. I might not have been born with wine in my blood, but at least I had the good sense to put it there at a very early age. I stared at a weird bird that was hovering in the sky, in the distance. It was like a little baby pterodactyl, coasting in wide, swooping ovals. I thought about how this story—the first involving me and wine—set up the relationship I'd been having with wine during my entire adult life.

Wine! Yeah! Wine! I am going to drink this wine . . . then that other wine! What about this wine, what kind is it? Oh, who cares, why not drink this wine, too! There sure are a lot of wineglasses around, and they are full of wine that I want to drink. God, this is so much fun! I feel like it's time to sit down now. I'm a bit tired! But that doesn't mean I should stop drinking the

*wine from these wineglasses! FUN! That person is looking at me
funny. And those people over there seem like they might be talk-
ing about me. Well, screw them! Top me off a little? GREAT!
I love this—I mean, except for those asshole gossips in the corner.
I haven't tried that red wine with the different label—what's it
called again? Château something something? Right, no matter!
Fill me UP! I am having so many interesting thoughts right now.
I'm dizzy! What was I just saying? I have to go to the bathroom.
Whoa! I'm fine, sometimes I trip a little when I'm in heels. NO,
I DON'T NEED YOUR HELP! Don't touch me. GOOD
TIMES!! Pass me that glass. Hahahahahaha! What were you
saying? NO. NO. I SAID DO NOT TOUCH ME I AM
FINE. Where the hell is the bathroom? GOD!*

We approached a sign for a gas station.

"Let's pull over," he said.

"We don't need gas." I tapped the plastic containing the
speedometer and odometer and the other meters.

"I want coffee. And nougat. I want to eat so much
nougat."

The sign said *"Pétrole"* and *"Nougat de Montélimar."* A gas
and nougat station. My father used to bring home great slabs
of it when I was a child. He would make sure to buy the
kind that came wrapped in a dark red bow. He would present it to me with a flourish, pulling it out from under a pile
of yacht club sweaters in his suitcase. After thanking him
with my most convincing hug, I would march it up to my
room and place it on my small desk, waiting for the moment
when he would walk in, take it, and walk out, immediately

cracking open the plastic. I didn't like nougat. It was the point of contact I loved.

I dumped a handful of coins into the Nescafé dispenser in the gas station's massive gift shop/convenience store. My father stared at the wall of nougat, eventually selecting the third-largest bar available. We returned to the car and continued south.

"What about you?" I asked.

"What about me what?" he asked.

"What about the first time you had wine?"

"Mine was just as traumatic as yours, Toots." Crumbs of pistachio and flecks of nougat coated his lap.

"Go. Tell me."

"*Eet* was two years after the end of World War Two. My father decided to put me in Scouts. *'Tu vas être un homme,'* he said. I was eight and chubby. The troop went on a lot of hikes, you know? This is what Scouts did. It also cost the organization very little money, which was good. One day in August—one of those oppressive days with lots of *beeg* heat—the troop was taking its afternoon hike. I was stuck somewhere in the middle of the pack, close to a group of older boys who seemed to be sharing an inside joke. I wanted to be there, with them. So I walked faster and hovered around them until they finally noticed me. They nodded to each other, laughing a little. Then they handed me a dirty canteen and ordered, 'Drink. When you walk with us, you're a man.' I thought, *Good! I am here to be exactly that, a man!* I took the canteen. The sun was boiling, I was very thirsty. There was no wind that day, and I'd had no water all afternoon. But there was no water in that canteen. Instead, there was a boiling hot treacly syrup—the cheapest red wine you can imagine. I didn't want to disappoint them, so I just drank and drank until the canteen was empty."

"Did you die of death?" This was an ancient inside joke resurrected spontaneously, but it caused a twang of pain to burst inside me. I shifted uncomfortably, immediately regretting the joke.

"No, Tootsie, I did not. An hour later, I woke up," he said. "I felt like . . . It felt like . . . *Eet* was like . . ."

"Like a bowling ball had been implanted in your head and there was a disco inside that bowling ball and the whole thing was trying to expand its way out of your skull," I finished.

"Yes. Nice image, Tolstoya."

I giggled stupidly.

"So, I woke with the troop standing over me. The older boys were laughing. My poor virginal liver! I was not a man, I was a boy, and I was a boy filled with the shame of not being a man."

"Poor little Dad."

"I said I would never drink again. I did not, until my downfall." He took a dramatic breath.

I nervously switched lanes to bypass a truck that had jack-knifed on the road. *Stupid death dumb driving joke idiot no death jokes while driving stupid tiny car on big road stupid stupid. Scrambled eggs brain.* I gripped the wheel hard.

"Don't you want to hear about my downfall?"

"Yeah. Yeah, of course. You saw I had to pass that truck, right? And the ambulances? And the police cars? You saw all that, right?"

"I don't care about those things. I want to tell you my story," he said, blind to my white knuckles.

"You are a ridiculous human being sometimes." I reached out and grabbed his shoulder. By squeezing it, I thought he might sense my nerves and complete the acrostic of my emotions. *How do you tell your father you do not want him to die?*

"*You* are a *reediculous* human being," he countered, smiling, unaware.

"Obviously I am a ridiculous human being, I am made of parts of you."

"True. Here. Listen. My downfall happened in April of 1960. I was twenty-one years old, living in Montreal, working for Air France in the catering division."

"And you got drunk and fell down." *Just keep cracking jokes until you're okay.*

"You're almost right. I mean, I never recovered," he said. "I have actually never really fully stood upright since." I glanced at his bum knee. He went on.

"That year, Air France switched its long courier fleet from conventional planes—Lockheed Super Constellations, big four-engine propeller-driven planes—to jets . . . Boeing 707s. Before the *sweetch*, a trip across the North Atlantic from Paris to Montreal would have taken eighteen hours.

There were stopovers in Shannon, Ireland, and Gander, NewFOUNDland . . ." His accent caused him to trip over the name. "NEWfoundLAND . . ." He stopped again, knitting his brow. "Toots?"

"Newfund-land," I said, enunciating deliberately. *You are in control.*

"Yes. *Newfundland.* So, with the new jets, the same trip took only seven hours. The inaugural flights in the new airplanes were reserved for Air France's most important customers. There were movie stars, sports legends, politicians, businessmen. The first-class cabin carried thirty-four passengers, the economy cabin one hundred and seven."

I marveled at his aptitude for detail.

"*Zee* food was prepared in the kitchen at Paris's Orly Airport by a team of chefs—old, knowledgeable pros. The Air France chefs were ordered to cook enough to feed a hundred and fifty travelers. We called them *les goinfres,* 'the eaters.' But just in case, they usually prepared enough food to feed two hundred and ten passengers. This was a time when plane food really meant something. The meals began with fresh beluga caviar. Then foie gras in aspic, followed by Roscoff lobster medallions with fresh mayonnaise. Next they were served seared veal chops in cream sauce with chanterelles, and beef tenderloin in Marchand de Vin sauce. After that, a *petite salade rafraîchie.* The meal ended with a tray of thirty cheeses from Androuët, the greatest *fromager* in Paris. And then a selection of little tarts and cakes. Each dish was accompanied with wine. To drink, they began with champagne, either Krug Grande Cuvée or Taittinger Comtes de Champagne. Then some white Grands Crus from Burgundy, sometimes Bâtard-Montrachet, sometimes Bienvenues-Bâtard-Montrachet or even, from time to time, the Montrachet Marquis de Laguiche." He uttered the last name in a halting whisper.

"What is that wine?"

"Oh, Tou Tou. It's such a wine. One of the most prestigious wines. It's been made in Puligny by the Marquis de Laguiche family since the fourteenth century. Today, certain vintages of Laguiche retail for around a thousand dollars."

"Do we have any in the cellar?"

"Yes."

"Give them to me."

"One day."

I let out a little groan. "Keep going!" I demanded.

"Then there were reds from Bordeaux, all Grands Crus, mostly from the 1953 and 1955 vintages—elegant years. With the cheese, some champagne—a nice Moët—to clean the palate, then harder stuff, generally Armagnac, and cigars to finish."

"So it was like a sort of Bacchanalian game of Russian roulette."

"What do you mean?"

"These are the dreams of which heart attacks were made!" I shouted.

"Yes! Exactly! At the end of the first Atlantic crossing

in the 707, more than a hundred and fifty bottles had been drained. We called them the cadavers . . . And that's only wine. Remember the hard liquor—vodka, Armagnac, Cognac, Scotch. When the flight landed, Air France personnel were on the ground, ready with a half-dozen stretchers to unload the passengers. Most were drunk as stones."

"That's not an expression."

"It doesn't matter. They were drunk. Torpid. Once they were gone, we climbed into the cabin, which was full of oily smells and smoke, and began the cleanup."

"And so?"

"You know what the writer Alphonse Daudet said, Tou Tou," he said.

"Uh, no."

" 'Quand le vin est tiré, il faut le boire.' "

"When the wine has been poured, it must be drunk," I responded.

"My twenty-one-year-old palate was almost virginal. I hadn't had anything to drink since Scouts, right? The purity, the seduction, of these wines was immediate and overwhelming. If you are born with a musical ear, you will take to Mozart instantaneously. If you are born with a receptive palate, you will have the same expérience déterminante."

"Not necessarily right away, though." I sighed moodily.

"With me, it was instantaneous," he said, unaware that I'd descended into a small, disheartened spiral. "I picked through the spoils, and gathered a half-empty Krug, the generous ends of two Grands Crus Bordeaux, and some food. Heavy, pearly spoonfuls of the wet, glistening caviar. Leftover meats, coated in their shiny opulent sauces . . . a bit of *la petite* salad, a piece of Camembert, some tarts. I placed them all in a bag and set them aside until my shift ended. Then I got on a bus, sat in religious silence until it stopped at McGill Park, stepped off the bus, chose a tree, sat down under its branches, laid out my feast, and in the cool spring air under a cool pink sky, I fell in love." He fell silent.

"That's a lucky story. Romantic." I allowed myself to relax again, if only for a moment. Because then, this:

"Did I ever tell you about the time I saw a woman getting fucked by a donkey?"

This made me laugh violently. I accidentally let the car veer into the oncoming lane, then straightened it out.

"No, no, you didn't tell me about the time you saw a woman getting fucked by a donkey."

"It was in Beirut, in a cabaret. I walked in, and there she was, getting fucked by a donkey in a harness. There was a small man at her side, holding a can of oil, painting the donkey's penis with a brush."

"I have no words," I said.

"You're not supposed to. You know what?" he asked with a sudden, strange solemnity.

"No. What?"

"I would like to buy a donkey."

"Why do you want to buy a donkey?"

"Because they are hardworking. Smart. They take a lot of shit."

"Like me."

"Like you, from me. But with you, it is too late. I have failed you. I want to atone for my sins by being good to a donkey."

"You haven't failed me!"

"Well, I still want that donkey."

A big fuzzy sun was dangling low as the landscape changed once again from highway to yellow green fields with their orderly rows of vines. We both hushed up. Despite all their gnarly sky grabbing, their weird, wild, Medusa-like shapes, perceiving the vines was no longer causing my stomach to feel as if it were filled with a bag of squirming piglets. We'd arrived in Burgundy. *Please make this the site of my own determining experience.*

I remembered for no reason a small triumph in my father's cellar. He'd been cradling a bottle in each hand, thrusting one out into my face, pulling it back, then thrusting the other into my face. The bottle on the left had sloped, feminine shoulders; the bottle on the right had square, masculine shoulders. As his right hand thrust forward, he'd asked me to identify what region the bottle came from.

"Bordeaux," I'd said.

"Très bien, ma grande."

The left hand moved.

"Bourgogne."

"Très bien, ma grande!"

We checked into the hotel. As I hauled our bags up the wide, winding staircase to our rooms on the second floor, I noticed a public computer. A black PC. *Internet access. Jesus Christ. Internet access. Matthew access.* As my father strode off down the hall, I let the bags in my left hand plop to the floor. I pulled out the cell phone and checked again for the envelope icon. The screen was empty, save for the date and the time.

Oh fuck. Don't ruin Burgundy with this crap.

I unfroze myself and marched along to my room, jamming my plastic key into the electronic reader.

"We'll go for a walk now, eh, Tou Tou?" My father was standing at the door of his own room.

It was evening, and the town had finished up its work for the day. We zigzagged through the tight abandoned streets, passing a row of stone houses, a vineyard, a clothesline with soggy rumpled pants. The day's work was all around us, especially under us, squishing into the rubber of our soles, staining the pale gray asphalt with bloodlike streaks. It was a delicious murder scene. My father lifted his foot and stretched out his leg toward me, like a karate man.

"Look!" His voice was as close to a squeal as tonally possible.

"Hey, juicefeet."

"That is at least twenty dollars' worth of Pinot Noir."

"How do you know it's Pinot Noir?" I asked, distracted.

"Tootsie, please, we are in Burgundy. Everything is Pinot Noir. And all the whites are made from Chardonnay."

"Right, right," I responded. "Sorry. I wasn't thinking. It's all Pinot and Chardonnay."

He veered off course into someone's vineyard. I followed, watching the grape skins accumulate around the edges of the soles of my boots. *Organic spats.* We ate grapes for a while. He, silent. Me, on another hyperbolic plane. I'd gone back to thinking about the computer and the phone and all of it.

"What are you thinking about?" My father was watching me.

I studied his face dumbly, not wanting to bring up Matthew again, searching for a quip or question to adequately fill the silence.

"Peacock tail!"

"What about it?"

"Describe it to me."

When we'd do Burgundy tastings, he would refer to the effect of the wine on his palate as a peacock's tail.

"It's a difficult grape, Pinot Noir. Thin skin, *eet eez* susceptible to disease. *Ce sont des vins de méditation . . .* these are truly the most meditative wines on earth . . . André Simon, Harry Waugh, these great wine connoisseurs called the effect of the Pinot Noir the peacock's tail . . . When you dr—"

You are a selfish person. You are not a criminal, but you are selfish. Sure, you can make a compelling case for yourself to him. You can continue to mine his love and indulge in it unilaterally. Explain what happened at the tasting with Nast; how you breathed deeply and the feeling of the wine in your mouth lasted and lasted, even though you'd swallowed it already. And how then, the words came.

Just ask for a little more time to breathe, so that truer feelings will develop. Ones that will last and last. Buy yourself some more time with him. Prove to him and yourself that you are not ruined and rotten and incapable.

I became disgusted with myself, with how much I needed. *Pathetic. Manipulative. Cowardly.*

"We should quit stuffing our faces," my father said, poking me on the shoulder, "or someone will see and throw our asses out of here." He tossed the last of his handful of grapes and they squished melodramatically against a stone, bursting easily.

Pinot Noir. Thin skins.

After dinner, we had a cocktail in the quiet bar off the lobby. We hugged good night at the door to my father's room. When it clicked shut, I turned on my heels and skittered down the hall to the computer. The light was warm and dim and had no calming effect on my stomach, which felt as if it were tacitly declaring insurrection. I couldn't help myself—my thin skin and I just couldn't help ourselves. Surely he'd written to me. Sensing that maybe his text messages weren't crossing over to a cell phone in France, he must have decided that it was a better idea to e-mail me directly. I logged into my e-mail account—there was nothing from him. I scanned my instant message contact list. He was online. I double-tapped the mouse and opened a message window.

"are you there?" I typed.

Nothing. No movement.

"hey," I prodded. "are you mad at me or something? i've been texting you."

I felt desperate. My midsection was throbbing with stress pangs.

"i miss you."

The window turned red and told me this person was no longer online and had not received my last message.

chapter ten

My father had a surprise for me. He had just announced this over our third and final coffee of the morning. We were picking bread crumbs off our plates with our fingertips. The sun was strong, the caffeine was detonating in my head, I was eager for the surprise and the day's tasting.

When I'd returned to my room after the fruitless computer communication attempt, I'd sat cross-legged on the bed and meditated on my progress over the last few days. It had been without epiphany, but steady and honest. I tried to concentrate on the idea of subjectivity—of wine and people—and the innumerable variables that inform our experience with them. One inconsistency could throw everything off-kilter: A good bottle of wine that is left in the backseat of a car to roll around or cook in the sun will likely turn to vinegar. Bad conditions can do the same to relationships.

I'd resigned myself to stop acting in bad faith with respect to my situation with Matthew. And I'd started, gingerly, to let myself off the hook for failing to find my language with him. There was no 100-point Parker scale for human affection.

"The Pinot Noir is a tricky bastard," my father said.

"He is a thin-skinned little fucker," I replied.

"He is known as the heartbreak grape, because he will break a winemaker's heart."

"He is the tortured child genius of the varietal world." We were both laughing.

"There is a universe of potential in that grape. Like you, my Tou Tou. He has a disarming personality. To drink a good Pinot Noir from here is to be captivated. There's a subtle power and complexity to it. But it is not a resilient grape. Its skin is delicate, it is prone to sickness and rot."

"Thank you, I think?"

"Ultimately, if a Pinot Noir is hit by a blast of cold air at the wrong time, or an afternoon of humidity without an evening of dryness, it suffers greatly. Its life can change in an instant." He reached over his plate of ham scraps and cheese rind and pinched my index finger. *Is he getting at what I think he's getting at?*

Fearful of descending into a moment of sobriety, I began riffing as fast as I could.

"Like, if an action movie was made about grapes, and it was set in the slums of Baltimore or Flint, Michigan, and the main character was a street-fighting grape who became embroiled in a back-alley rumble situation and was about to have the living crap kicked out of him by a gang of tough fruits—like rambutans or, God forbid, pineapples—that grape would *not* want to be rolling with a crew of Pinot Noirs. Those Pinot Noirs wouldn't step up—no way. Pinot Noir grapes would rather be curled up on a cushy velvet divan poring over Baudelaire's *Les fleurs du mal* or weeping over a Rachmaninoff concerto. Forget those grapes! What our street-fighting main character grape would need is an entourage with muscle—brawny, brass-knuckle grapes. Ones who have gang colors and a special walk. Cabernet Sauvignons. From Australia, if possible. One of the dumb thug Cabernet Sauvignon grapes with no discerning characteristics, save for their ability to fight it out—not with finesse, only muscle—just like all the other dumb thug Cabernet Sauvignons. Right? Right, Dad?"

"True. You're right. Sometimes when you are not at home I will go into the cellar and read Baudelaire to the Burgundies."

"What's the surprise?"

"It's a surprise."

The drive to the surprise took very little time. Down another pastoral road covered in vines, winding through dusty rectangular homes of beige stucco and squat terra-cotta flowerpots, over cobbled roads, up a hill flanked by tilled fields.

"WHERE DID YOU PUT THE CAMERA, TOOTSIE?? I WANT TO TAKE A PICTURE OF THE SURPRISE." My father was out of breath from rummaging around the car in his patented ineffective manner: lifting every liftable object in sight, while looking straight ahead, his face contorted with a sort of faraway concern that is distantly related to the knowledge that he'll never find what he's looking for, because he's not really looking. This is his subtle manner of delegating; he flails around and whines until someone jumps in and does the finding.

"Dad, it's right here." I plucked the little case from beneath his left thigh.

"Okay. Let's go."

The morning was blue and spotted with smoky clouds. There was no wind, no people, no movement. Only gently snaking rows of greenery sloping ahead of us, up, up, up, until the greenness collided with the sky. In front of us, a tall cross was guarding the entrance to the vineyard.

He entered it with a funny look of devotion on his face. I followed.

"This is it," he said.

"This is what?"

"It. The vineyard of Romanée Conti."

"Uh-huh," I said, standing dumbly with the camera.

"These vines make the best wine in the world."

The vines had already been harvested, so we stood around and ate *grappillons*—the leftover grapes that were too small and runty to be picked. I clicked a picture of him with a mouthful, he took three of me. We rustled the leaves around some more, foraging. Pouring another small handful into my mouth, I was hit.

"OH!" I gagged and coughed up a tiny grape. It sat at the back of my throat. I took a breath and swallowed it again.

"What?"

"My birthday bottle—"

"Yes!"

"Is from this vineyard."

"Yes."

"This one right here."

"Yes."

"Like, this grape"—I spat it into my palm and peered down at it—"could be the great-great-grandkid of one of the grapes that went into my birthday bottle."

"Yes."

"Stop saying yes," I said.

"Yes."

"Huh."

"What do you think about the surprise?" he asked.

"It's really something, Dad."

I chewed another little grape carefully. When he'd presented me with my bottle, I'd been an awkward seventeen-year-old. His movements had been so sure—we'd walked down to the cellar together. He'd scanned one of the wine stands in the middle of the room and swiftly slid out an old-looking bottle with a simple white label with "La Romanée, 1979" printed on it in black letters. Placing it in the cradle of my hands, he'd rolled it so that the label was facing him. The glass was cold and gritty with dust. Joyfully and generously, he'd written, "Tou Tou's birthday bottle," and said,

"This will be ready for you when you are a woman. I don't care what you drink this with, or who you drink this with. You can have this with a hamburger. I don't care. It's yours. When you choose to open it, just make sure you're happy."

I looked over at him from across a row of vines. "I think this is a terrific surprise. The best."

He continued to eat, but my throat was tight with love.

Five minutes later, I exclaimed again. "Oh!"

"Yes?"

"And Romanée Conti was the vineyard where they harvested . . ." I paused. "What year was the year where everything was all screwed up and—"

"Nineteen seventy-five."

Like magic, I brushed the dust off a story I remembered only sketches of—a story I always enjoyed and had attempted to recount in proper company, where it came out vague and lackluster, devoid of punch line: *So, in—eh, France . . . I can't recall what year, exactly, maybe the eighties . . . maybe '82? Anyway, for some reason or another, the harvest got all screwed up and the harvesters couldn't, you know . . . harvest properly . . . And they didn't know what to do . . . it was a famous house, one of the big ones in . . . I think, like, Bordeaux or Burgundy? . . . Ehh . . .*

"Remind me?" I prodded him.

"In 1975, most of the country got clobbered by terrible weather. It lasted from May to September. Sticky, humid, rainy. Awful. The berries on most of the vines were mutants. The grapes were bloated with water. They were sickly and sad. So this left the managers of Romanée Conti with a

tough decision: Make the wine and risk hurting their repu-
tation, or scrap the crop."

"But they came up with a solution, right? They picked the
grapes individually?"

"Exactly. The harvesters were sent out to comb through
each bunch and pick only the healthy berries. Some bunches
had only one or two salvageable grapes. The vineyard produced a tenth of what it normally would in a year—a few
hundred bottles as opposed to a few thousand. The 1975
vintage turned out to be the essence of what is produced in
this area. It was not a classic vintage, but it did justice to its
name."

This story filled me with comfort.

"Hey, Dad."

"Oui, ma grande?"

"Do you think viticulturists here are more psychotic than
other viticulturists? I mean psychotic in a nice way. Obsessed. Obsessed in the same way you'd be if I'd been born
more delicate than other babies, like if I'd had a skull made
of pressboard? Am I making sense? Is this a stupid question?"

"Pre-eh-ess-boo-ard?" He drew out the word, trying to
find its meaning.

"Forget the pressbo—"

"No. The question is not stupid. But I don't know. You
know, I met Lalou Bize-Leroy a few years ago, she had me
in for a tasting."

"I remember." Lalou Bize-Leroy used to be one of the

two owners of Domaine Romanée Conti and is still one of the most fabulously talented winemakers in the world.

"You remember what?"

"I remember you telling me you met Lalou Bize-Leroy. I know who she is."

"Who is she?"

His question caused me to shrink down to little-girl size. Slightly annoyed, I answered: "She used to be one of the two owners of DRC."

"Right, bravo. Before we did the tasting, she took me for a tour of the vineyard. Standard procedure. She is a tiny, intense woman, always surrounded by her adoring dogs from an exotic breed—pedigrees that date back to Charles le Téméraire, the greatest of the warring dukes of Burgundy."

"Mm. Go on."

"Standing with her in the vineyard, I saw a change overcome her. She was becoming a high priestess before my eyes. She pointed up and said, 'See, the moon has to be there, in its fourth quarter, which is when we lay the organic fertilizer.' She does not say 'blood of Christ,' but that's what she means when she talks about the earth, the *sol nourissier,* the origin of life. She looks at me and says, '*La puissance de la vie . . .*' and trails off. She was searching for something in me, an understanding, a nod of recognition. But I'm not a member of this club. She has before her a guy who is partial to what comes out of a decently pressed Pinot Noir. I am not one of the enlightened ones, who understand the moon and its relationship with the earth, or the *sol nourissier*. So she smiles and says, 'I think it's time for a little *dégustation* in the cellar, no?' I have become, in her eyes, a mortal."

He is mortal. He is a mortal. I simultaneously felt worse and better.

"That's pretty incredible," I said.

"What's incredible?"

"To dedicate your whole life to loving something you have no ultimate control over."

"That is what it is to be a winemaker."

"And a parent?"

"Same thing."

"Thank you," I said.

He smiled. "Thank you for being here."

On the walk back to the car, I tried to sort things out. He and I seemed to be reaching a place of adult honesty. I reminded myself to be patient with the other subjects—the big ones—my accident, how he *had* failed me, in a way, with his words and actions in the days thereafter. How I wished he had more of an intuitive understanding of my agony. How this prevented me from asking for his help with my feelings toward Matthew and how I worried I was cursed with his terribly timed selfishness. How all of this was eclipsed one million times over by my huge love for him and my much huger fear of his death. *Honesty does not flow trippingly off the tongue.*

Once seated in the car, my father asked for the cell phone. As I pulled it out, I masochistically scanned the display for that goddamned little envelope I'd been waiting for.

It was there.

Oh God.

It was there, plain and proud. A tiny rectangle containing a fat inverted isosceles triangle.

Christ.

"Tootsie, the phone, please."

"One second, Dad. There's a message. Let me check what it says." My voice wobbled out of my throat, which felt as if it had been smacked with an iron pipe.

Fingers fumbling along the digits, I opened the message. It was from Matthew. It read:

"it's too bad."

My brain began screaming into a canyon. *It's too bad? WHAT'S TOO BAD?* I clicked over to the "sent messages" folder; there was nothing. *The phone doesn't save sent messages? What kind of piece of crap phone doesn't save sent messages? What the FUCK did I say in the last message? Elephants. The colonial elephant wallpaper. That's what's too bad? That I was cooped up in a luxury room with aesthetically threatening wallpaper? Or it's too bad about us? About my tricks? About my slatternly ways? About our relationship? About the condition of his condition? About the condition or our condition? About the melting of the polar ice caps? About the Khmer Rouge regime? About American foreign policy? ABOUT WHAT????*

"Tootsie, the phone."

My father dialed numbers while I used them to count backward. An amorphous panic overtook me, as if I were on a crazy game show that involved trying to survive a haunted house where there is an ax murderer in any one of the closets. I counted backward. *Ten, nine, eight, seven . . . What's the use. What a worthless tip, that is, to count backward from ten. Count backward from ten, don't worry, be good to yourself, take it easy, stay positive, don't be so hard on yourself. OH? REALLY? Why, THANK YOU! I hadn't thought of those options . . . Whatever would I do without you and your Chicken Soup for the Neurotic's Soul HORSE SHIT PLATITUDES?*

No. Really, though. There is a better-than-average chance that this is about wallpaper and paste and pachyderms and men in hats with monocles.

I fixed my eyes on the quiet panorama outside the windshield. I heaved in as much oxygen as my lungs could handle. Best-case scenario: My quip about the elephants was weak and warranted an equally tepid response. And that he knew about all the guys I had slept with while keeping him and his terrible love as my primary self-worth food source, but his heart remained solid and intact. Worst-case scenario: He's a mess of human tissue and it's my fault and now I will be obliged to admit that I want him to feel good not because he deserves to feel good, but because it would alleviate my tremendous guilt about what I've done to him, and how that is the most brutal articulation of my pitiable character.

Fuck. I hope it is the elephants. Also: I cannot control this situation from this continent.

"*Bonjour?*" a tinny voice came out the receiver. My father was holding the phone in front of his face, as one would a baby who has just vomited on itself. I steadied myself and thought about the nice, neat metaphor of the DRC harvest of 1975. Good berries amid a ruined harvest.

"Oui, bonjour, madame. Ici Philippe Borel."

"Bonjour, M. Borel." The tinny voice belonged to a woman. An impatient woman.

"Is this Madame Nudant?"

"Yes . . . ?"

"Ah, hello. I'm calling to confirm our appointment with you at two this afternoon."

"Yes. Yes. Two o'clock."

"So two o'clock it is."

"We're right in the middle of the harvest." Mme. Nudant was huffy.

"Of course."

"We're very busy, you know," she barked, "but of course we're very much looking forward to receiving you."

My father glanced over at me. I mimed a big shrug and chuckled a little.

"Madame Nudant, it's not imperative we come. We understand it's harvesttime, and how busy you are. We're happy to call off the visit, truly."

"I wouldn't think of it," she said flatly. "We're just scrambling because of the harvest."

"Yes, the harvest. Naturally it's terribly busy. You're sure?"

"Absolutely sure. We wouldn't have it any other way. But please respect how overworked we are at this time of year."

My hands were now clamped around my mouth, choking what was coming from my diaphragm. I rolled down the window, opened the door, and exited the car as quietly as I could. I let out a few whispery giggles, then stuck my head back into the car.

"No, but please, madame, we can cancel."

"No, monsieur, we wouldn't have it. You will come. But we're very busy."

"We will make it a short visit. We thank you so much for your kindness."

"*A bientôt.*"

"*A bientôt. Merci infiniment. Merci, merci, au rev*—"

The phone beeped, she hung up.

"What the HELL was that?" I said. "What passion. What passivity! What aggression . . . What passionate-passive-aggression . . . passionivitygression . . ." I started laughing again.

"She's out of her mind," he said.

"Well, Dad, you know, it's harvest season, and she's very busy."

"Am I crazy? Did I not suggest we cancel the visit three or four times?"

"About that."

"Was I the only one who heard that? *Venez, venez, monsieur, non, j'insiste . . .*"

"She was adamant."

"She was, wasn't she?"

"She was."

Pulling into the cobbled drive, I noticed my father's expression change.

"This woman does not want us here. She does not want us bothering her. This is going to suck," he intoned.

"Oh no. Don't say that."

"We will not be treated well here. I do not want to be in a place where I am not treated well."

"It'll be fine, I'm sure. Please, Dad. Cheer up."

That's the game. Tha-aat's the game. He's doing it. I thought about how he used to do it not only at my tennis games, but at my basketball games as well. It enraged my mother —there are stories of him sitting in the stands with the same aloof fatalism he showed at my outmatched tennis matches—amid the rah-rah apple-cheeked American parents, watching me play exhibition games with my community basketball team in Dallas (the Stratoblasters!). These games were always shamefully low-scoring—I was eight—and if our team gave up the ball, say, twice, my father would look at my mother gravely and state, "That's the game." And we would lose. We were terrible; many of us thought dribbling was optional.

Standing in front of the stone enclosure surrounding the Nudant property, my father reached out to ring the bell with a look on his face that said, *I'm not here.* I wanted to hang a DO NOT DISTURB sign around his neck.

The wooden gate flung open, and there she was, the embodiment of what her voice had indicated: black-stained hands, fraying collared shirt under a splattered navy blue sweater, rubber boots chunky with mud, hair blown horizontal. Glancing at my father's unblinking face, I stretched out a champion smile, the broadest, sparkliest smile I could muster.

"Bonjour, Madame Nud—"

"Oui, oui, les Borels, entrez, entrez."

I felt like scum. I continued to beam. I was the sun. I was a heat-seeking missile of positivity. I denied myself all the doubts and worries and dread that I was having at Romanée Conti and focused on my massively overstretched mouth. I was a paper crane, perfectly folded, not allowing the rain to take away my structural integrity.

She led us out to the vineyard behind the house.

"These are the vines. They have been harvested. These are part of the AOC, obviously. Do you know how that works?" she asked. *Oh God*. Now I was an army of paper cranes.

"Mostly!" I nodded, hoping to seem curious, but not so curious that she would grow annoyed with having to explain AOC in detail.

"So you know, then, that AOC stands for *appellation d'origine contrôlée?*"

"Indeed."

"Here, it is more complicated than anywhere else."

"Practically impenetrable!" I agreed.

"As you know, in most regions, wines are classified according to what château they've come from. Château XYZ produces a bottle of wine, that wine is given the name of the Château XYZ. You were born into the Borel family, you are given the name Borel."

"Right, Borel, sure!"

"But in Burgundy, the classifications are based on geography and *terroir*—the exact area in which that bottle of wine is made. If you were a bottle of wine from Burgundy, your name would be . . ."

Worrying that she had forgotten my name, hoping my father would reengage, I blurted, "Kathryn Toronto General Hospital, room A-187, or something. What room was I born in, Dad?" *I made this joke for you, you ghost of a human.*

My father shrugged. She went on, unsmiling.

"The bottle is given the name of the village in which the vineyard is located, and that name is displayed prominently on the label. But not all vineyards are classified as AOC, and there are different quality classifications within them. And there are blends from various villages . . ."

Reeling, I tried to follow along but became lost and quietly sad. *Why can't we just do a tasting? This morning, I had all of the words to describe this wine. I wanted to describe myself, through the wine, to my father. And now we're doing none of this, and this woman is not being very nice to me, and he is not protecting me.*

"Do you understand what I am telling you about the system?"

"Sure I understand," I said, unsure of which part of her monologue she was referring to. "But of course I don't understand the idea of AOC as much as you understand it, so maybe you can explain it a little more?"

She sighed. *I can't win. Today I will settle for being a loser.*

"*Vous voyez, AOC* . . ." She launched into more of an

explanation, sighing and placing her knuckles on her hips. Her eyes flickered. *Did she just roll her eyes?* As I was watching her body language, I had lost the thread. Now I was well and properly lost. Scrambling to seem as though I were following her thread, I concentrated on picking up my social cues. When her voice hit an upswing, I said, "aHA!" or, *"A bon!"*

He is not protecting me, like he didn't know how to protect me from that lecherous man in Alsace . . . like he didn't know how to protect me from the emotional fallout after the accident.

"Allez, je vous montre la cave."

We whirled through the cellar, her arms pointed this way— "This is our family tree, we've been making wine since the fifteenth century . . ." And that way—"Those bottles there, the ones under the barrels, those are extremely old, they're full of mystery wine that we share with friends, for fun, we open them on special occasions, *with friends* . . ." She looked pointedly at my father and me—we were not her friends, and she would not be sharing this mystery wine with us, for fun. This was not fun. For anyone. My father had still not opened his mouth. I was putting myself through Expression Charades worthy of a goddamn Oscar, eyes huge, lips parted in delight, nodding as if I were a bobblehead in a bumper car.

Mme. Nudant had whipped out a wine thief—a small glass sampling tube—and she was thieving wine from one of the barrels, filling us in on the vintage, the growing conditions, yapping nervously as she shot the liquid into glasses and handed them to me and my mute companion. Swirl, sniff, glug, I threw it down the hatch. She watched me for one second, waiting for a descriptor or a reaction, but I gave her none of my metaphors. *There's no point.* She went on to the next barrel, pulled out two more glasses and more explanation. Up the stairs, over to the vats where the wine was heating. She was stabbing her finger into a chart specifying the various temperatures at which the wine would heat, when—oh, dear Lord, have mercy—her husband and son walked in.

"Monsieur et Mademoiselle Borel?" M. Nudant asked.

"Oui, Monsieur Nudant?" My father spoke. *Oh, now you're not a monk anymore?*

"Bonjour, bienvenue. Mon fils, Guillaume." We all shook hands. Mme. Nudant saw her chance to escape and hurried by us.

"So, my wife has given you the tour?" he asked.

"Yes. It was generous of you to meet with us. It's clear you're in the thick of it," my father responded. His quiet violence had disappeared.

"It was our pleasure, really," he said sincerely. "Why don't you come into the kitchen for a cup of coffee. The harvesters are eating lunch."

"Perfect," my father said. *Perfect?* We followed M. Nudant.

The lunch table was a joyous clattering mob scene of family tree foliage—Grandma Nudant, Guillaume, Papa Nudant, six or seven ruddy-faced harvesters, a young aspiring winemaker from New Zealand who had come to Burgundy to apprentice. Grandma served us cups of instant coffee. Suddenly, I was wise to what was going on—with Mme. Nudant, at least. For her, we hadn't interrupted the harvest, we'd interrupted a kind of birth. Something deeply personal. We were strangers who had swanned into the hospital as the baby was crowning. As we drained our small porcelain cups, my father chatted graciously with the group. Relieved but confused with his behavior, I said nothing. I clattered my cup down on its dish and shifted, signaling that I was ready to go. My father rose, then I rose. M. Nudant held up his hand and rushed out of the kitchen, returning with two beautiful bottles for us to take with us. As we thanked him, I bowed my head in tacit apology.

I carried the bottles, trailing my father, feeling silenced and slighted by him. I kicked the tips of my toes into the pebbly driveway, sending small rocks in the direction of his ankles, hoping they would fall into the backs of his shoes and cause him discomfort. A similar discomfort to what I'd just endured. But I wasn't really kicking hard enough to get them in there. I watched his body sway back and forth, as nonchalant as could be. I measured my movements against his—they were choppy and stiff, like those of a windup metal toy. Huffing, I plowed my toe hard into the ground. A spray of pebbles cascaded into the backs of his legs. He didn't turn around.

chapter eleven

In the car, I am thinking.

I can yell.

I CAN YELL. I have license to do it, so I will.

Okay. I am just about to yell at you, DAD.

We were driving south, toward Côtes-du-Rhône, in a silence that was stony on my end, neutral on his. I planned on yelling something to the effect of, "SO SHE DIDN'T TREAT YOU WELL, WHAT ABOUT HELPING ME OUT?" Not quite sharp enough. "YOU CAN BE SO SELFISH SOMETIMES." Not specific enough to carry any resonance. I'd been mulling this over for a good couple of hours, while making sure my driving was stunningly adroit, so that when I gave him my yell, it would be very jarring for him.

"I should have died here in 1944," he said matter-of-factly.

DAMMIT. I shifted the hot pan of my injury to a back burner.

"Here? Like, where here?" I was gauging how seriously to take the comment.

"Over there." He pointed out the window, across the stretch of highway we were rolling along, at a cluster of drab taupe-colored downtown buildings.

"Oh."

"Do you want to hear the story?" he asked.

"No, I'm not that interested. But thank you for offering." I was half kidding, still grasping at the vestiges of my anger.

"You're welcome."

I turned on the radio and feigned interest by cocking my head to the side and arranging my eyes and mouth into the Face of Intense Contemplation. My father was sneaking glances at me in the rearview mirror. I stuck my neck in and out in time to the music.

"Dad."

"Yesssss?" he said.

"Jesus, I'm joking around with you." I bashed my palm into the power button. The car went silent.

"Dad?"

"Yes?"

"I don't like it when you treat the idea of your death lightly." *There. It isn't quite "I'm fucking scared of losing you before I've found you . . ." But we're at least on the dartboard.*

"But it's the truth."

I thought of him outside the car, bouncing off the right

side of it. My face flushed. I slowed down the car to the correct speed limit.

"Okay, okay. It's the truth. Tell me the story, then. I assume your almost dying has to do with the war, right? And the Jewish organization? And the kids . . ." I prodded helpfully. I felt ashamed of having made the joke about not wanting to listen.

"Yes. Your grandfather . . ."

"René . . . good old René." I pronounced this "Reenee"—an Anglicization of his name, which became his nickname during the last ten years of his life. He'd called me *ma puce*—my flea—and we'd always had a soulful bond. So much so that it didn't bug me when I'd receive letters from him that would include copies of the correspondence I'd sent him—the spelling and syntactic mistakes circled in red pen.

"So you remember his story with OSE."

"Organisation de secours aux enfants."

"No. *Oeuvre* de secours aux enfants. It was founded at the beginning of World War One, by a big mountain of a man called Lazarus Gurwich. His nickname was Le Rhinocéros."

"Good name."

"You remember that Albert Einstein was its honorary president."

"No."

"Well, he was. René began working in the OSE headquarters in 1934—we were based in Paris. His colleagues were Jewish doctors, intellectuals, social activists, most of whom had, at one point, been chased out of their towns, their villages, sometimes their countries. When the war hit in 1939, René refused to abandon them, even though this was, as one would say, not *exactly* the best time to be connected with an organization like this. Trucks holding hundreds of orphaned Jewish children started arriving in France in 1939 and 1940. OSE's sole mission was to keep them as far away from the hands of the Nazis as possible. The organization set up a network of safe houses. It rented buildings and old châteaux. The kids went to live in the countryside, with families who were against the war. OSE gave them fake names and fake documents. It set up 'summer camps.' The children were given survival training and kept fit."

"René was an accountant, yes?"

"Right. His job was to be a *payeur*. This meant he traveled between Switzerland and France. In Switzerland, he would pick up money that had been sent to its banks by Jewish-American support groups. Then he'd get on the train back to France and distribute the money to keep the organization running. Every trip was *vahree* dangerous. If the Gestapo had caught him, he would have been dead."

"And you?"

"By 1944, we'd moved from Paris to Montpelier to Vic-sur-Cère. Then to Chambéry and Chabannes. And eventually here, in Lyon. We had to stay mobile. The Gestapo was getting better at knowing where OSE was carrying out its work. In February, officers raided the Chambéry headquarters, arresting the head of the group, Alain Mossé, and all his colleagues. Your grandfather was in the office, too, in the back, quietly going over the books. But before the men had a chance to throw him in the truck, Mossé pleaded with them, explaining that my grandfather was just the French accountant—a paid employee—not a member of OSE. They asked him to prove his gentility."

"Yes yes yes. You've told me bits of this. So he had to drop his pants, right?" I said, slightly ashamed that this was the part that I remembered so clearly.

"He dropped his pants and the officers left him alone. His secretary, Simone Epstein—who was 'Simone Estienne' on her false identity card—was left alone, too. *Right* before the raid, she had run into a nun selling small hand-painted cards. On them were pictures of saints. She bought a few and put them in her purse. So because of her ID and those little paintings, how could she possibly be Jewish? The Gestapo let her go."

"Whoa."

"Mossé was an elegant, intellectual man with soft manners. He always had a piece of chocolate for me when he came to our house for dinner. Two days after that raid, he was tortured by Alois Brunner . . ."

"Sorry . . . he was . . ."

"The head of the Drancy internment camp. In those two days at the Chambéry prison, Mossé was able to smuggle out notes to three members of OSE. René was one of them. The note said the Gestapo knew of OSE's 'summer camp' in the region. Officers were going to raid the area. But when they did, the camp was gone. Mossé was sent to Auschwitz. You're following me?"

"Of course I am." I felt insulted. *Did he mean to do that?*

"By the time we were pushed into Lyon, René was doing his work for OSE out of our tiny apartment. We had very little food. There were air raids. Across the street lived Klaus Barbie, the head of the Gestapo of Lyon. Barbie was known *affectionately* as the Butcher of Lyon. He was the man who tortured Jean Moulin . . ."

"Big-time French Resistance guy," I jumped in, trying to prove myself.

"You got it. Barbie was responsible for the deaths of thousands. That April, he ordered that forty-four Jewish children be rounded up from an orphanage east of Lyon, at Izieu, and sent to Auschwitz. Not one child survived."

We drove in silence for a minute.

"And so . . ."

"On the twenty-eighth of May, your grandmother Fernande Léa stood in the staircase of the apartment, trying to make her little boy hurry up."

"You."

"Me. I was complaining of a sore throat and fever. I'd done this a thousand times. Half the time, she would give in to me and allow me to skip school. I would then make a miraculous recovery and be allowed to go outside and play with my marbles."

"All of which you still had."

"Ha. Funny girl. That day, she couldn't give in to me. She

had to shop for groceries, not easy when food is limited. She did not want me there—it would have been a handicap. It was eight o'clock. We were leaving the house, *point final*. As we walked into the street, we heard air raid sirens. The U.S. Air Force had been dropping bombs on bridges, railway yards, and factories for the last few weeks—most of the people in the neighborhood were used to the blasts. I remember the airplanes very well: They were silver flakes against the blue blue sky. Then, a big noise—a *whoosh* and the smack of an explosion. My mother thought a bomb must have landed somewhere near the avenue—she said this out loud to me."

"But it hadn't."

"No. After she dropped me off, and after her shopping, she walked home. When she turned the corner onto our street, Avenue Berthelot, she was stopped by police officers and firefighters. The blast had been a military mistake—the bomb had dropped directly into the residential zone, onto our home."

"Oh Christ. It was gone."

"Everything was gone. The building was a stump made of stone. Everyone who had been spending the morning inside was dead. René had left an hour earlier to meet a *passeur*—they were moving another group of Jewish kids out of the region. We had also left the house earlier than usual. By some fluke, we all survived."

I said nothing.

"Anyway, Tootsie, that's the story. If she had allowed me to stay home from school that day . . . Well . . ." He paused.

"You and I would not be having this conversation right now," I responded.

"Exactly," he said.

I sat there maneuvering the car from lane to lane, passing and being passed, thinking about timing and death. A Dinah Washington song popped into my head, and I thought the lyrics were all right but also kind of all wrong. *Twenty-four little hours make a difference, sure. But so do twenty-four little minutes, or seconds.* Because of them, my father was here. Because of them, I was a killer. I thought of those awful seconds it took for me to draw the link between the crunching sound that came from the right side of the car and death. Those minutes I stared at the old man's shoulder rising and falling. Those days that passed as I waited for an update from the police. Those months that flowed afterward that caused me to transform into this person, right now.

As Peter and I pulled a U-turn out of the accident scene, the two-liter bottles of tonic water—which I had bought to mix with the gin we were to drink that night—rolled off the backseat and lolled jerkily around, thumping against the door. I remember looking back at them accusingly, knowing that if I had stopped at another grocery store, or had paid for them using cash instead of a credit card, or had located the soda aisle more efficiently, or had not spent a minute deciding between Schweppes or Canada Dry, or, or, or, or, or, or, or . . . that *I* would not be having this conversation with myself, on this highway. All decisions, and whether they are made twenty-four seconds before or after, push us out of death's way or directly into its path. *It's a platitudinous dichotomy. Boring, cliché. But its effects are not. My father is freed by it, I am bound and bedraggled.*

"Your face *eez* a sad face, Tootsie."

"I'm just thinking about the glory of good timing and the nonglory of bad timing. And how they define a person's life. It feels like a prison sometimes."

"You are talking about your accident."

"That is indeed what I am talking about."

"You feel like you did not deserve to have this happen to you."

"No," I said haltingly, scared of causing another disconnect between us. I swallowed hard and went on, "No, not really. I don't believe in 'deserving,' really. Do I deserve everything? Yes. Do I deserve nothing? Yes. What gets me perturbed is this thing that happened, this humongous, life-changing thing, did not happen for a reason. It happened for no reason. It happened because I spent too much time at the grocery store choosing tonic water. And if I hadn't, what? Someone else would have killed him? He would have crossed the street safely? But . . . whether it's his fault or my fault or our combined faults or no one's fault, I am a girl who becomes very sad. And depressed. And I think about death a *lot*, you know?" I added nothing more. I could see him withdrawing.

"Not really," he said. I took in his face, his inscrutable face. *Where does he go?* My urge to yell at him had returned with fury. *Now it is your turn to listen to my story of why I am like this. I wanted to tell you this nicely in Burgundy, but now we are here and you will listen to me.* It was my turn to orate.

"I've thought about it a *lot*. My own. *Yours.* What I would do if our family died, and I was left all alone. Because I get *depressed*, Dad. And I go to crazy, terrible places in my depression. I lose all sense of reality and *time*. Do you know what it's like to no longer believe in *TIME*? That your entire life will now be a cave of agony? *FOREVER?* And I have no resources to pull on that allow me to convince myself that I will ever feel any other way. No *resources,* Dad. Even though there's all this evidence to the contrary. I can't even *believe* in time and *empirical* evidence. I reject reality. Do you *get* that? Do you? Like, you've seen the sun rise seven thousand times and you are so fucked up that you cannot access the information that indicates the sun will, based on empirical near certainty, rise tomorrow?" *You must understand why you are obligated to protect me.*

"Calm down, my Tootsie. You're driving too fast." The speedometer was vibrating at 145. All at once, my anger shifted to an overwhelming brew of terror, culpability, guilt. I slowed down the car.

He reached out his arm and squeezed my shoulder. "Sweet, sensitive Tootsie," he said.

"God. I'm sorry. I'm selfish. You tell me a story about the war and poverty and escaping a bomb—and I do all *this*." What he'd shown me of his pain hung like a big, basking late afternoon shadow over my own. Mine felt like a speck.

Some nothingness. A dried-up crumble of sauce. I brushed it aside—refused to give it credence.

One silly, lone tear dumped out of my right eye.

"Do you want to hear a sad and unlucky story? It might make you feel better. You know, it will give you some relativity."

"How sad and unlucky?" I wondered if I needed more relativity. But he wanted to share.

"C'est une histoire vraiment déprimante."

I let him share.

"Yes. A sad story. Excellent." I did not want to think about what I'd just said about the accident, about my depression.

"See, your grandfather stayed with OSE until the winter of 1948. We had come back to Paris—it was a different city, *bien sûr.* Decay, destruction, the shadows of war were still hovering over France. In February of 1949, he made a decision for the family. He had a dream—"

"That his children would be judged not by the color of their skin, but by the content of their character?" I interrupted.

"Heh. Yes. Any*waaaaay.* His idea was to go to Switzerland. For him, because of his work, it was a land that represented peace. Security and stability. It was the land of his ancestors. He had a connection with it. And he had found an inn on the shore of Lake Geneva, in Vevey. His dream was to buy the property—we would become innkeepers."

"Do you think that's why you had an interest in hotels?"

"Non. Pas du tout."

"Oh."

"He liquidated his bank account and put the cash into a briefcase. He booked a night train from Paris to Geneva, a trip he had taken many times. He arrived at the *gare*, located his train, went to his compartment, and dropped off his suitcase and his briefcase on the luggage rack, as usual. The night porter arrived and asked to make up his bed, as usual. He left his compartment to have a cigarette on the platform, as usual. He got back to his compartment a few minutes later."

"As usual," I finished.

"Exactly as usual. At some point, he looked up at the luggage rack. His suitcase was there, the briefcase had disappeared. A train thief had come and gone. Did he understand that his life had changed forever, once again? The briefcase contained his life savings. He was meeting with a notary in Geneva to purchase the inn. No savings, no meeting, no inn."

"Fuuuuuuucking hell."

"Yes, Tou Tou. Fucking hell is right. And there was another surprise waiting for him at home. Mimi was on her way." Mimi is the nickname of my aunt, Marie-Françoise.

"C'est pas vrai."

"C'est vrai." My father was chuckling.

"But why . . . I mean, why in the world . . . Like . . . Jesus . . . What *possessed* him to leave the briefcase alone?"

"Oh, Tootsen, who knows, *hein*? He was a dreamer, your grandfather. This made him careless, irresponsible sometimes."

"And how did he tell you guys?"

"I was away, in the Alps. He waited until I got back. I don't remember much, though I *do* remember his calmness. He explained the probable impact on our lives, but that we were not to worry, that we would save face. But if you think about it, there was everything to be worried about. He was forty-six, he had no money, he had no job, and it was post-war France . . ."

"So the prospects were not exactly abundant."

"No. Abundant, I believe, would be the wrong word to describe our prospects."

"And then?"

"The family had a hard time for two years as France rebuilt. Over those two years, René put together a new dream. He would immigrate to Canada, begin a new life for us, and then send for us when he was set up over there. He left us in October of 1951. He boarded a plane and landed in Montreal. Then he took a train to Toronto. An old Russian woman named Sorele took him in. Another member of OSE had organized the whole trip and this house where he would stay. Lys was Sorele's great-niece and had been writing to her great-aunt about the arrival of this man, a tall Parisian—not a Jew, but a man of honor. I remember him telling me that on their first evening together, Sorele made an abominable dish of poached carp. He complained about how jellied the fish was. They ate the jellied fish while Sorele spoke to him of childhood memories of the pogroms, the Cossacks, the burning of the old Jewish ghetto. He told her stories of Paris, of our family. He told her about the murder of his friends and colleagues. Good people. Undeserving people. They became friends."

I drove steadily.

"He stayed under Sorele's roof for a little while. Eventually, he had enough money to rent *une chambre minuscule* above a shop on Spadina Avenue, in Toronto's Jewish community. OSE helped him get a job as a floor salesman in a large fabric store."

"There were no accounting jobs for him."

"No. It was a pathetic job," my father said, "for a man who was as much of a salesman as I am a nuclear physicist."

"When did you guys get there?"

"About twelve months later. We took a boat. Your grandmother was seasick to the point of immobility. I was sexually harassed by a young priest on the ship—"

"Oh, Dad," I cried, uncomfortable.

He continued without pausing, "Right away your grandfather became very sick with emphysema. He was forced to quit his job. Your grandmother had to stay at home with the baby—your aunt Mimi. My parents suspected, I think, that I was an *imbécile*, so they sent me to a nearby trade school. There I went during the day. I was the only boy in my class. I learned how to use a typewriter and cook elementary meat and pasta dishes. When school was *feeneeshed*, I would walk to Bistro One-Two, where I worked at night, scrubbing pots. This was my life for four years."

I did an audit of my head. I no longer felt terror—I'd become engrossed in his story. He told it so well, with such accuracy. In Rémy Gresser's cellar, he'd been able to shape the wine with his language right away. Gasoline. Perfect. Meanwhile I was all laborious breathing and wine gurgling and word fumbling. *But at least you've begun. Shapes are emerging from your primordial ooze! You are feeling! There is real hope for you!*

"Dad, so you told me this story."

"I did."

"But how do you feel about all of it?"

"I move on, Tootsie."

"You just move on."

"That's right. I just *mooooove* on."

I wondered if my feelings were stupid.

"Ah, Tootsen, look up," he said.

I looked up and around; we were in the Alps. The change of scenery caused my eyebrows to twitch.

"The Alps!" Mountains had exploded around us in the last nanosecond, like an earthquake in reverse. I fell silent at the weight of it all.

"No," my dad said.

"No what?"

"No, these aren't the Alps. These are the *Préalpes*."

"The Prealps. I did not know there was such a thing."

It was as if a herd of great mossy stegosauruses had popped up around the road. We drove among the dinosaurs, large and small, for forty minutes, until we were back where we were always arriving: fields filled with grapes. But they did not unravel levelly in front of us, as I was accustomed to. Instead,

the scene was a page out of a Dr. Seuss book. We were surrounded by corn yellow hills, all ascending brazenly at impossible gradations. Clinging to the earth for dear life were rows
of vines. Their branches were twisted and wild and seemed
to be shouting over the road at the vines on the opposite hill,
"Guys, hey, GUYS! Can you freakin' believe this?!!?" And
the vines on the opposite hill were all like, "Yeah, man, what
the *hell* is going on? I'm freakin' Neil Armstrong over here!"

My father seemed to sense my amazement, likely by way
of my gaping mouth. I could have swallowed a pumpkin.

"This, Tootsen, is the Côte Rôtie," he explained.

"The Roasted Hill."

"Prized wines are made from the grapes that grow on
these roasted hills. The vines face a perfect south-southwest
orientation. The sun is amplified by the reflection of the big
river." He pointed hither and thither.

"What's the river?"

"The Rhône River, Tootsie. Come on. Think."

"Right. Côtes-du-Rhône." *Ouch.*

"This is the kingdom of Syrah, in the reds, and Viognier,
in the whites. It is sun-drenched wine. Opulent, rich, volup-
tuous, velvety."

I tried harder: "They're like the young beach bums who
spend all their time hanging out and soaking up vitamin
D. They are grapes with a healthy seaside glow. Blond hair,
sticky from the ocean. Bouncy, cheerful grapes who are part
of the macrobiotic movement and do hot yoga."

"Yes. Good. Something like that. They stand alone at the

top of the northern Rhône hierarchy. They are divided in two sections. Côte Brune, Côte Blonde. The Brune's soil is clay, rich in iron oxide. The Blonde's is lighter in color. Mainly chalk," he said. "I read somewhere the names came from Maugiron, the first lord of Ampuis under Henri the Third. He had two daughters, one blond, one a brunette."

"They must be a bitch to harvest. The quads and glutes on the harvesters must be out of this world." I decided that one of the tasks I would accomplish before my own death was to have some hot times with a Côte Rôtie harvester.

"Accidents have happened on these hills. All the harvesting is done by hand. Machines cannot deal with these monstrous *terraces*. They're ancient. They date back to Roman times," he said.

Another hour of snaking through skinny roads and tiny towns and patient fields and we arrived in Sainte Cécile-Les-Vignes, a bitty town of two thousand Frenchmen. I parked in a lush cobbled courtyard, flipped to the appropriate page of our itinerary, and scanned down the page to find the name of our contact.

"Aubert," I said aloud.

"What did you say?"

"What did I say about what?"

"The name you said."

"I said 'Aubert,'" I repeated. "René Aubert. The owner. Of this. This place."

"Right."

"I think that's him there." A tall, ectomorphic man strode

toward the car with spindly arms and legs. He was handsome and spiderlike.

We unpacked ourselves from the car. Immediately, my hair was blown off my shoulders. It whipped into my eyeballs and stuck to my freshly glossed lips. I peeled it back into place with no luck. A lock snapped me again right in the eye.

"*YEOW!* That wind is *so annoying.*" When I blinked, my right lid felt as if it had been dredged in sand. I gathered up the thrashing mess and tied it back into a ponytail.

"*Salutations!*" Aubert's eyebrow was cocked. He seemed to be sizing us up. I thought of Nudant. *God, I hope he's done with the harvest.* Self-conscious about my windswept appearance, I patted down the natty lumps and smiled with my sticky mouth.

Aubert led us through the showroom and store for his wines, Domaine de la Présidente, then through an old, polished door into his office. *What an enclave!* I half expected two servant women to appear, wearing velvet bikinis, ready with tiny spoons heaped with oozing morsels of triple-cream cheeses and platters of grapes they'd peeled with their long, polished nails. It is also possible I was fantasizing about food-bearing hussies because I was starving from fueling my body for the last four hours only with those stinking little plastic cups of gas station Nescafé.

He motioned for us to sit. His smile was broad and sly, his eyes crinkled and slit, his chin pointed up, ready for a bird to come and perch upon it. He raised a fist, then let it fall and bounce off his desk like a judge bringing order to his court.

"Alors," he said, "what it is that you expect from me?" *So direct! He is princelike. He is a wonderful, witty, cruel, and joyous Renaissance prince.*

My father took a breath, but I cut in before he had a chance to say anything.

"This is our first stop in Côtes-du-Rhône. We were just talking about the historical origins of the Côte Blonde and Côte Brune. Maugrignon, you know."

"You mean Maugiron," Aubert said. My cheeks grew hot. My father's shoulders tightened in the slightest of cringes.

"That's what I said, no?" *Dig dig dig.*

"Permit me to give you the background on the domaine."

"Of course," I said, so quickly defeated, wishing we were doing a tasting. I was spent from the drive and off my game. I'd seen the operation in Alsace. I wasn't interested in the mechanics of winemaking anymore. I wanted to *feel some feelings* through *wine* and therefore allow myself to metaphorically *stick my hand up my father's nose and feel his strange electric blue glowing brain before time ran out.*

"In 1968, my father, Max, bought the domaine. Max was the mayor of Sainte-Cécile-Les-Vignes, and I was intent on working among the vines from a very young age. We began with sixty hectares. I worked very hard. Now the domaine has doubled and . . ."

Aubert's voice was a patchy radio signal. I caught bits here and there but was focused mainly on staring at a row of thick old volumes on an inset shelf above his head. *Oh, you are a fool.* He and my father were bonding over France's lost innocence. The chances of me knowing anything about France's lost innocence were low. *You could barely remember the uncomplicated name of a man who essentially founded the most prestigious terroirs in the region.*

"Wine is the story of a generation. It is the manifestation of nature and psychology," Aubert said. I felt like yelling for the third time today. *I KNOW IT IS THE MANIFESTATION OF NATURE AND PSYCHOLOGY—THAT IS THE WHOLE POINT OF THIS TRIP.*

Now my father and Aubert were laughing at something I had not caught.

"*Kathryn!*" Aubert said. I jerked up. When my mother is angry, she says, "*Kathryn!*" loudly in French, and I know I'm in for it.

"*Oui, Monsieur Aubert?*"

"Have you ever tasted a wine that's only been fermenting for a few days? Would you like to see the operation?" he asked.

"*Oui, j'aimerais bien ça, Monsieur Aubert,*" I said.

As soon as we were back in the courtyard, I received another hair lashing in the other eye.

"*YEOOOW!*"

Aubert laughed. *What's so funny, Aubert?* I contained my impulse to kick at the ground like a petulant child.

"*C'est le mistral,*" he said. He looked at me with one eyebrow slanted and went off in the direction of what looked like a low-lying barn. We followed.

Inside, there was that characteristic smell of bubbling fruit and warm, blooming yeast. He filled two glasses, one with a cloudy gold liquid and the other with a cloudy pink liquid. I sipped the yellow; it was a mouthful of the tropics: super-ripe pineapples all drippy and honey sweet. The other was the best spiked fruit punch.

"The white is Viognier," Aubert said.

"Strange," I said.

"Why?" My dad looked at me.

"Because the Viogniers I've had have always been more flowery than fruity," I explained.

"C'est intéressant, hein?" Aubert said.

He was being cryptic, withholding information, maybe waiting for my questions. I *did* want to ask him a question—I was desperate to do a tasting. But I was too unsure about protocol and too distracted to ask questions and diligently take notes, to take more of these notes I'd been jotting into my red desk calendar, these quips and philosophies from viticulturists and vintners and sommeliers. Could Aubert explain why a bunch of Viognier grapes—in their first week of fermentation, when the yeast is industriously converting the sugar into alcohol—tastes like pineapples, only to end up, a year later, tasting like flowers? Probably. But I was tired! It's magic! Magic need not be deconstructed! MAGIC! Just because I enjoy driving a Saab doesn't mean I have to ask a mechanic to take the Saab apart in front of my eyes to show me why I like driving the Saab, right?! Can't I just taste the Saab? I mean, *drive* the Saab? And taste the wine?

"Oui, c'est intéressant." I waited, let a pregnant pause pass,

not too pregnant, first trimester, probably, then went on. *"Très interéssant."* I mustered as much authority as I could and injected it into the latter part of my response, hoping to defend myself from a possible follow-up question.

We moved on to the red punch. Aubert listed the grapes. The list was long: *Mourverdre. Syrah. Grenache. Cinsault . . .*

"What a party!" I said. *Party punch.*

"Mais oui, Kathryn . . . Bien sûr. On est a Châteauneuf-du-Pape." He chuckled. Of course, he says, we are in Châteauneuf-du-Pape, after all.

He whisked our drained glasses out of our hands and marched them over to a big sink. I look pleadingly at my dad.

"Toots, Châteauneuf-du-Pape wines are all *assemblage.* Lots of grapes in every bottle. Major, major *assemblage.*" He said this under his breath, quickly.

"Assemblage. Got it. An assembly. A bunch of different types of grapes, I know. But when do you think we're going to do a tasting?"

Aubert returned before my father could say anything. He announced, *"Venez,"* and let himself out the back door.

In the vineyard, with my hair swirling all around me as though I'd just jumped out of a goddamn plane, I decided that I would change my strategy. *Seduce him with questions until he has no choice but to let us taste his wines. Take those scraps of information and rework them into a flock of good questions. I am ready. I have shimmied into a pair of short shorts. I have laced up*

my sprinter's cleats. I have stretched. I am limber. I am in the blocks.
I fire the starter's pistol. And I'm off.

"What field are we standing in?"

"These are Grenache," Aubert said.

"And over there?" I weather-vane-spun to the left, pointing over a road of packed dirt and rocks to another field.

"Syrah."

"And when the grapes are picked and put into the fermentation vats, are they done together or separately?"

"Separately, naturally," he said.

"So you can mix them after? To control the taste? Like combining red and blue to make purple, and adding more blue for a darker purple?"

"Eh bien, c'e—"

"Like, if you were to put a bunch of babies from different families into the same room and just let them spend their first crucial months together, the lot of them would turn into some weird amalgam toddler with a collective nondescript personality—traits so mixed up you'd never be able to tell which families the babies originally came from." I noticed Aubert's eyebrows were cocked again, in the shape of the pointed roofs of neighboring houses.

"I think your color analogy was more accurate," Aubert said.

"Oh. All right, then."

"We just came from Burgundy," my father offered by way of explanation.

"Alors, une dégustation?" Aubert led us the direction of the wine showroom.

"Oui, avec plaisir!" I said.

I jumped in the air and kicked my heels to the side, as a joke just for my dad. He reached out and grabbed the nape of my neck. I felt like a good kitten.

Aubert uncorked five bottles, set out a long row of tasting glasses, and filled them generously. We chewed the liquid in the first glass in silence. It came from a bottle called Les Partides, from 2000.

"This one is a Grenache-Syrah blend. We leave the Grenache on the vine, *en surmaturité,* so that the hot weather can dry them. This concentrates their flavor. We do this to give the wine structure."

I wasn't inspired to say anything, so I grabbed for the next glass: a 2003, Grenache, Cinsault, and a bit of Syrah.

"Oh, it tastes just like *birthday cake.*"

"OUI, oui! Le cake," Aubert agreed. "Kathryn, it's the first time I've seen you become excited today."

I blushed. "Sorry," I said shamefully, "it was a long drive, for me."

"No, no . . . no apologies. *C'est de la vraie passion!"* He looked over at my father and said, *"Votre fille est charmante, intelligente."* He was suddenly interested. *"Quelles sont vos passions?"*

My passions?

"In general?"

"In general, about wine, whatever."

I thought about how to appropriately answer his question. My father was gazing at me with pride.

Death, no, jokes, no, boys, no, masochism, no, sweater vests, no, well-toasted toast in the shape of France, no, drinking, no, fronting, no, running, maybe, German philosophy . . .

"I studied German philosophers in university. I suppose that was a passion." I uttered this in a vague way, feeling self-conscious.

"Which ones?"

"I loved Schlegel a lot. His *Philosophical Fragments* especially." *You sort of sound like a wanker, dude.*

"Why?"

"Because I like the idea of a tiny phrase, a small thought, conveying more than the individual meaning of the words put together."

"Explain."

"Well, I've never liked lists—" I stopped and self-corrected, "I mean, I use them all the time when I'm going nuts . . . But in theory, I hate them, because they reduce grand concepts, or moments in history, or people, or even wine, down to something that is small. When you sum up the items in a list, it never amounts to the original concept." I went on, gathering momentum, "But with Schlegel's *Fragments,* there's this radiant moment that goes beyond its own boundaries."

"It expands," my father said. He was telling me he was engaged. I gained more speed.

"Right. It expands and expands. Like with wine. This cake wine is not just Grenache, Cinsault, and Syrah . . ."

"It's everything around it, too, all the growth around it," Aubert said.

"YES. It's not only the soil and the weather patterns and the manner in which it was treated in the bottle. It lives individually, then lives in your mouth, and in my mouth, and in my dad's mouth . . . And there, it doesn't just live, but it *reacts*, and not only chemically to our taste buds. It reacts and relates to the person whose mouth it's in, to how they're feeling that day, to their memories and the company they're in."

Aubert and my father were beaming at me. *Holy fuck. Nice one, Borel.*

"You must have lunch with me."

We feasted happily on a meal served by Aubert's grandmotherly cook. A salad dotted with boiled eggs, the yolks orange and pleasantly runny. Ground grayish pink meats in aspic with pistachio studs. Soup, more meat, bright steamed vegetables, the carrots carefully turned and glazed. Dessert, coffee.

We all said a good-bye worthy of *Le Bal Crillon des Débutantes,* full of flourish and grace. One kiss, two kiss. Dainty waving, demure smiles. My father and I slammed our car doors, *clack clack.* I checked my side and rearview mirrors and turned the car out of the courtyard.

"You're a slam dunk, Tootsen," my father said. Then he laughed crazily, 100 percent proud.

"Oh, man. Thanks. That was . . . That was really a thing, you know? We should go out somewhere good tonight. You and me. And champagne," I blathered happily, grabbing the itinerary from his hands, ready to do all the driving and all the navigating. We passed a sign that told us we were going in the right direction—in the direction of Suze-la-Rousse. The magic-hour sun flashed off the silvery whiteness of the sign, blinding me for a moment. Dumbly exhilarated, I stepped into the accelerator and cracked the window to let in the crazy viny wind. I breathed in. A tiny ghost of Aubert's cakey wine worked its way back into my mouth. My father tapped the glass of his window, indicating that I should turn down a packed dirt road. I slowed down and turned the wheel. The road turned into another courtyard, this time covered in smooth gray pebbles. I parked and squinted at the main house of the bed-and-breakfast—an adorable stack of stones with big cutout windows.

"I *theenk* there is a great restaurant Blondie and I once went to around here. Somewhere. Not that close, but close. It's a thirty-minute drive away, maybe. I can't remember exactly. Good for you, Toots?"

"Yes. Excellent. It will be perfect."

We unfolded ourselves from the car and began to stretch.

chapter twelve

I am going to vomit all over the cobblestones, right outside
that hell of a restaurant. Just spray them down with every drop
of Aubert's wine and hope that it is that gold-faced waitress
who will have to clean it up, because we are technically still
on the restaurant's property. It will be red, and it will look like
the blood that formed in a pool around the old man's wrinkly
ear, lying in the street on the early afternoon of that frigid gray
February day. My hands are on my knees. For the shortest of
moments, I try to summon the laugh my father released in the
car just two hours ago. The one that said, *I'm listening to you,
because you are a grown woman and my daughter and you are good
and worthy of respect and I am proud to be your father.*

I kill that thought dead.

My father is watching me. I do not register what emotion
is on his face; I am in flames.

You must get away from him now.

Knowing he cannot keep up with me, I barrel down the hill toward the car. I am resigned to put the fear of fucking God in this man. I will make him feel the way I do: powerless.

When I scream up the hill and the lights first flash on his shape, his face is immediately bathed in bright white light. His eyes are as wide as flapjacks.

"I'M HUNGRY. GET IN."

I will yell.

He opens the car door and swings his body around quickly, fastening his seat belt.

I reel the car around so fast that his head slams back into the headrest. The tires squeal and the smell of burning rubber floats in.

"You are sixty-six years old, and you understand NOTHING," I yell.

My father does not react.

"You are going to die. You know that, right? You are going to *die*. And you will have given nothing to me. A bunch of monologues about stuff I don't give a *shit* about. A handful of moments that were of *your* doing, that *you* planned without ever asking me what *I* wanted to do."

My heart speeds as quick as the car. *I need all this air in here. I need more than all this air.*

I open a window and breathe the way I would if a doctor were holding a stethoscope to my chest.

The wind batters its way into the car and causes my hair to whip around as it did in Aubert's field.

"You are going to die in a way that is just as sudden and ugly as when I hit that old man. And then I'll be left with nothing and more nothing. A bunch of stories that you did not share—a bunch of stories which you told from your soapbox. Stories with no lessons for *me* that I could use in *my* life. Oh, and your cellar's worth of wine. Your thousand bottles. Your buddies. The ones you *actually* listened to, thought about, were intimate with. You can't remember my birthday, but you can tell me how many bottles of Clos des Mouches are in the basement. You studied the ullage of your bottles, smelled the corks, tasted your wines, took notes about their character. *What can you tell me about my character, Dad?* You yelled, *'That's the game!'* at my tennis matches, but you will fly over an ocean to a London auction to buy a bottle of wine that might have already turned to vinegar."

"That's not true," he says, his eyes on his lap.

"And you don't even *care* that I might be ruined. That the accident *changed my entire life.* It changed who I *am*, Dad. I am *unhappy all the time.* I *worry all the time.* You talk about almost dying in the war, and you don't make the connection that I am driving in a car, fast, on a highway and how that might make me feel *fucked up and scared because I think about you dying all the time.*"

Tears flow down my face. "And I don't know what happened with Philou and Marc, but I know they're mad at you because they feel you didn't do enough for them, either. I understand why Philou called you a good-time Charlie. I understand why religion seemed like a safer option for Marc. Because you don't understand that we are adults, and we too have seen and done REAL THINGS, and you turn us into little kids because you don't listen to ANY OF IT. You disengage. And then I turn into a stupid little kid because that is how my *father* sees me. He sees me as someone who is not worth listening to. But *I am worth listening to.* I resent you for that. I hate you for that. I *hate* you, Dad. DO YOU HEAR THIS?"

My breath becomes short. My breaths are those of a puppy who's just gone running after chasing a delicious-smelling animal. They click at each inhale. I look at him. He is scared. I am terrified of what I'm saying. *You didn't mean that last part. Now you are not being truthful.*

Fuck it.

My mind speeds along with the car. *This is it. I will no longer be his daughter. I can lose him before he loses me.* The space behind my eyes zooms and my stomach goes floppy. It's the vertiginous rush of desperate and ultimate freedom.

We reach an intersection. I do not know where to go.

"Choose," I demand.

"Wherever you want." His voice is a whisper.

"FINE, *DAD*."

I shudder and the vertiginous feeling widens in my stomach, chest, and head. My breath shortens further. It goes *ha-click-ha-click-ha-click-ha.* A half a second between every exhalation. A breath every quarter second. Squeezing my hands tight around the wheel—so tight that I feel the plastic grooves imprinting dents into the fattest part of my thumb pad—I cast my gaze far down the road, fixing it on a tree with a big fat trunk. It looks like a baobab tree, though I don't think there are any baobab trees in the south of France. *Whatever! Shut UP! The genus of the tree is not what's important right now. What's important is a fat trunk and a good deal of speed.*

Now, a decision. Shall I come up on this tree fast and then? Or shall I create a brief mood of foreboding by slowly veering into the oncoming lane and then?

With steady, committed wrists, I pull on the wheel. Left, left, a little to the left. The front of the car goes from facing twelve o'clock to eleven o'clock. I'm frustrated, though. There are no cars in the oncoming traffic lane. The tree that is thick like a baobab but not a baobab—when mixed with 115 kph—should be enough. Should. I don't know for sure. When it comes to cars and death, I only know that 55 kph will kill an old man.

My father is immobile.

I reposition the front of the car to a more dramatic angle. Eleven o'clock to ten o'clock.

My father's hands are now on the wheel. Tugging it in the opposite direction, he screams.

"TOOTSIE TOOTSIE TOOTSIE TOOTSIE TOOTSIE TOOTSIE STOP THE CAR PULL OVER PULL OVER STOP THE CAR DO IT NOW NOW

NOW NOW NOW NOW NOW NOW NOW NOW NOW NOW NOW NOW NOW!!!!!!!!!"

What the fuck. What the fuck. What the fuck. What the fuck have I done?

"WHAT THE FUCK IS WRONG WITH YOOOOOUUUUUUU?" His voice is tense, livid, crazy.

I whale on the brakes and fishtail to a stop on the gravel shoulder. I fling the door open so violently, it makes an angry squealing noise and bounces a few times. Then I jump out and stomp over to the other side of the car.

"*Jesus Christ.*" He mutters this as we cross paths behind the car, him moving toward the driver's seat, me toward that of the passenger. *Perfect. It takes a near death experience for him to offer, after eight hundred kilometers, to drive.*

"Are you okay?" he asks. His tone is low and flat.

It's his turn. He will receive my silence. I will give him a whole bottle of his bitter, rotten medicine. I keep mum.

"Tootsie. You are not okay."

I squeeze my lips into a line and rest the side of my forehead on the glass, looking up at the ugly sky.

He drives.

When we arrive in the town of Orange, he parallel parks near a bistro with an entrance like the mouth of a cave. I sit still as a stone. My father gets out of the car.

When he shuts his door, I press the button to my left. The doors go *th-thunk* and lock. His face appears at my window.

"Toots," he says impatiently, through the glass.

I stare straight ahead.

"Toots. Come on. Enough." He sounds exhausted.

From inside the glove compartment I remove Aubert's parting gift to us—a book on vinegar his sommelier had written—and leaf through it. I settle on a page and read the first three words of the same sentence over and over again.

"Fine, then." He walks a few paces; I watch him. He turns around, and my head shoots down again. He walks back to the window.

"Tootsie. You can't sit in the car like this. You must eat," he scolds.

My stomach rumbles. He is right. *Dammit.* I turn the page.

He raps on the window, using his thick gold wedding band to make an annoying clanking sound.

"Come on, Toots. I'm hungry." *He cares more about the food than to talk about what has happened. How can I share a meal with this man?*

I keep reading.

"You can't stay in here all night. You will go hungry. I don't want to eat alone." *For once, I don't care what you want.* I decide I will eat, but for myself. For *my* nourishment.

Organizing my face into the most spectacular display of contempt, I grab the handle and kick open the door so that it hits my father in the hip.

We have pizza and a bottle of wine. Sensing rottenness, our teapot-shaped waiter presents us with complimentary shots of Limoncello at the end of the meal. I drain mine, then grab my father's before he has the chance to drink it. He attempts conciliatory scraps of conversation. I rebuff them. He insists I eat the dessert he ordered; I shake my head in refusal.

Back at the hotel, he moves to hug me. Eluding his arms, I back up through the glass doors of my room, staring at him. All the while, my stomach churns and storms and froths.

"Good night, Tootsie. Thank you for eating with me tonight," he says, not able to meet my gaze. He pulls shut his door.

As my own door clicks behind me, I try to orient myself by focusing on specificities. I put on my pajamas and wrap myself up in the duvet. *What is happening? What now?* I roll over so that my face is thrust deep into the pillow and begin to howl.

This trip is making me lose more than I am gaining.

In order to stop crying, I clutch my torso with both arms, cutting off my breathing from the source. Dementedly, I sweep my arm around the side of the bed, searching for my satchel. I locate the phone and dial Matthew's phone number.

He picks up the phone on the third ring. He says hello the way he says hello.

"Hull-oh?"

"Oh, it's *you*," I say. I release a million cubic tons of air from my lungs.

"It's me," he agrees. The line makes him sound far away.

"It's *me*," I whimper.

"I know." I scan his tone for rage, for pain. I can't pick up anything.

"Matty."

"Kathryn." *That's my real name. My real, adult name.* In English, it sounds foreign. I start crying again.

"What are you calling about? Do you know how late it is here?"

"Matty. I said the most terrible things to my father tonight. I was so mad at him. And humiliated. He humiliated me in front of a waitress tonight at dinner. In front of the entire restaurant, even though I'd begged him not to. I begged and begged. But he ignored me and turned this tiny little-girl waitress into a pile of dust. And everyone in the restaurant was staring at us like we'd come from the asylum. He knocked over a chair. And then I tried to hit him with our car . . . and then I drove to Orange . . ." I start burbling, grabbing at the pieces of our evening and putting them into sequence for Matthew so that he could properly comfort me. "I mean, he really yelled, you know? And then I ran, and I drove, and I almost hit him . . . Why is he so bad at being a father? . . . He's going to die and he doesn't care enough to protect me from anything . . ." I pause to catch my breath and hear Matthew's steady breathing into the receiver of the phone.

"And so I went a little nuts, right . . . Saying all these things to him. But he wasn't listening, he didn't look like he was listening to anything, and so I tried to make him say something by trying to drive us into a tree."

"Kathryn? What the *hell*," he continues severely, "are you doing calling me and telling me this?"

You've lost him, too. You've done it now.

Petrified, I descend into weak babble. "I'm sorry. I'm sorry I'm calling. I'm homesick. I miss you. Tell me I don't suck."

He wants to be left alone. You have disrespected him.

"Is this the only reason you're calling? I have to order a pizza now."

"But how are things going?"

"Fine. You're not missing anything here." This he says quietly, carefully.

I lower my voice, too, and say, "Oh."

"Listen, Kathryn," he says, sounding as though he is choosing his words delicately. There is a pause. "I don't love you anymore."

My body goes still. I snap shut the phone. He'd separated the two parts of the last word and spoken them firmly, individually. *Any. More.* As though he'd been shaking his head while saying the syllables. As though he'd shaken me right out of his head, forever.

For the next seven hours, I watch the development of blue. The ultramarine blue of midnight . . . The dark sinking that happens at around three a.m., when everything becomes entombed in thick, dead black blue . . . The blue that's in the scene in the movie wherein two people must bury a corpse in the woods . . . Then, the cautious plum blue of dawn light.

The room brightens, the objects in it grow more defined. Inside here, inside me, it is the opposite. Inside, I have a blobby creeping sensation, as if a bike mechanic has rigged a nozzle to my stomach and he is slowly pumping me full of air. I am empty. But I am also becoming excruciatingly pressurized. As the day grew up, a very large conclusion dawned on me. I had taken advantage of him. All of him—more than just the Jell-O making and the key delivering—though that was part of it. I'd abused his dogged generosity, his piety of our love. I had used him.

I continue to lie in bed while the morning birds continue to scream their songs. *You are selfish, as selfish as he is.* I replay last night's events on a loop, and every time the loop begins again, I feel like my face is going to cave in, just cave into the back of my skull, through these sheets, through this bed. With all the violence I can muster, I kick off the bedclothes and starfish. It's still so early. Closing my sticky eyes, I stop the loop and divert my energy into orienting myself. I try to do it successfully this time. I do an inventory of beverages I would rather be drinking today. *I want orange juice. I want fresh-squeezed orange juice, definitely, and I would settle for certain brands found at the grocery store, though not the ones with so much pulp that it feels like you're drinking a glass of citrus-flavored sperm. Chocolate milk. In the five-hundred-milliliter container. I would prefer to drink chocolate milk out of a cardboard box. I would not care that the poorly waxed spout always gets all pink-tinged and saturated and floppy so that every time you take a sip, tiny wet balls of paper get stuck to the inside of your upper lip.*

I go to the bathroom and fill the clawed tub with hot water.

Give me any color of Gatorade. On the topic of aggressively colored drinks, I would also willingly consume Red Bull, TaB Energy, POWERade, and that fluorescent carbonated type that dyes your tongue the scariest shade of green. Perrier, with its menacing bubbles. Earl Grey tea with homogenized milk. Plain homo milk. An eight-dollar coffee from Starbucks. Tap water. Cooking sherry. French fry grease. The blood of twelve Vietnamese children. A glass of a syphilitic's urine. Coca-Cola. Anything. Just no more red wine.

Directing the shower nozzle toward my face, I blast myself with glacial water. It enhances my ice-cream headache.

Today, I will really and honestly puke if I have red wine.

As the ceiling fan *whoosh*es around, I make an inventory of pain. *My father, Matthew, the trip. I have reached the kind of saturation point adults reach when they decide they should take a night class in something they have no natural predilection for. These decisions are generally based on whims that are fueled by two dangerous mental states: self-affirming idealization ("I will learn how to become a Mexican chef because I can do anything!") and delusion ("It's never too late to become proficient in quantum mechanics!"). Family, love, wine. The correct execution of the recipes, the answers to the equations. Maybe they will elude me forever.*

And then, right on time, my father knocks at the door. I open it. Though I cannot feel it, the universe appears to be in order: He is standing on my patio dressed in nothing but a cream-colored towel and the eternally untied running shoes. In his right hand, a yellow Nike resistance elastic. He always brings this on trips.

"How are you? You look pale," he says neutrally. I remember what he said in the car, driving away from Burgundy. *I move on.*

"I didn't sleep."

"At all?"

"I don't think so. I talked to Matthew last night."

"Ah, you connected."

"Yes. On the phone. To say we connected is an overstatement. He told me he wasn't in love with me anymore."

"But, eh, it is you who broke up with him." He states this with zero emotion. My stomach begins to churn again. He is now doing chest extensions with the elastic, making choppy growling sounds every time he stretches out his arms.

"Sure, yes, I did, but it's not that simple. Dad, I've explained this to you already . . . Jesus . . ." I pause, searching for an outlet for my fury, which is going into its second bloom. Peering at his towel, I spit, *"Where are your pants?"*

"Rr. Rr. Eh. Rr. I am working out," he says.

"I can see that, but why aren't you working out in your room?"

"I wanted to see *eef* you were ready for breakfast. Rr. Eh. Rr."

"Yes. I am. I have pants on. I am dressed. But you're not, so I'm trying to figure out why you decided it was necessary to come and knock on my door to see if I was ready when you're at least a half hour away from being ready yourself. It doesn't make any *sense*."

He finishes his chest extensions and slowly turns to contemplate the vineyard. Where there was gold yesterday, there is now frost. It's gradually misting away in the washed-out morning sun.

"You see this sun?" he says.

"I see that sun," I snap. He ignores my bitchiness. *Is he ignoring me out of choice or incomprehension?*

"This is the sun that gave van Gogh paintings their light. Their luminosity. This region is famous for this sun. The way this sun shines, and the way the wind blows, makes the grapes healthy. It cleans them of the gray rot." The wind. *Le mistral.* That's what Aubert was laughing at. On another morning, I would want to make the connection out loud, so that he would notice and be pleased with me. Fuck it.

He pauses. "I want ham for breakfast," he concludes.

He walks distractedly back in the direction of his room.

We sit in the little pit bull lady's house, assembling our breakfast plates. Dozens of flies are perched, probably hatching eggs, all over the food: the spread of pink charcuterie, the rounds of soft yellow washed rind cheeses, the fresh crusty chunks of baguette, the jams and jellies, and the Frenchily requisite tub of oozing Nutella, its droopy chocolate-hazelnut folds studded with the crumbs of breakfasts past.

If today were better, I would be slathering gobs of the spread onto toast. I would be reveling in the wondrous notion that France, ostensibly, has been raising at least two generations' worth of children with the belief that the only civilized way to start a day is with enormous spoonfuls of a transcendent chocolate substance, one with the miraculous ability to blur the line between liquid and solid. I would be delighting in the bucolic landscape outside this beautiful restored barn, with its airy, creaky windows and splintered supporting beams. I would be poking little Camille—who is on the floor playing with a discarded box—in her little toddler belly. Thinking about the magnificent day ahead. Anticipating the first gluggy splash of rubescent wine in a balloon glass.

Instead I am watching my father eat ham. I am watching him eat ham with an intensity that is vicious and judgmental. Every time he reloads his plate with more ham, he absentmindedly waves off the flies, staring into the middle distance at nothing in particular. The room is mostly silent, save for Camille's cooing and my father's jaw, which makes a muffled popping sound when he clamps his molars shut.

I hate this pop. This man is unaware of the pop. How can he not be aware? The popping is in his jaw. His jaw is next to his ear. The sound is coming from a place that is on the same physical territory as the part of his body that absorbs sound. The man cannot hear.

His stare is unbearable, inscrutable. When he stares at nothing, he looks like a recently caught fish, still alive, but barely, in its last pathetic death flap, breathing poison air through its heaving gills, staring up calmly with a glossy eye that does not move, not a bit. My father's eyes are fixed, like the fish; they happen to be looking outward only because that is the direction they point, but he is not seeing anything. Or if he *is* seeing something, it is certainly not me.

I am in the car again, waiting. The car is not moving, because my father is looking for his *bréviaire*.

"Tootsie! Have you seen my *bréviaire*? I have lost it," he says, rooting through the backseat of the Citroën.

"You have lost it? I am shocked," I say.

"Thank you," he says.

"Has it ever occurred to you to put it in the same place?" I ask.

"*Thank* you," he says. The words are a gunshot. He gets what I'm doing but isn't acknowledging it.

The drive is silent for what feels like hours. There is some crunching of the little car's tires on the fat, loose gravel of the narrow *route départementale;* there is some cantankerous wind *whoosh*ing through the anorexic tops of the cypress trees.

"Why aren't you talking to me?" I prod.

"I have nothing to say," he says.

"Are you going to be this quiet when we get to the place? Because I'm *really* not in the mood today."

He's staring out the window, at the sky.

"I just feel like you don't even care about this conversation I had with Matthew last night. Like it bores you. Like it doesn't matter that I'm hurting. That I'm not myself. What is it about my situation that's making you act this way?" I skip around the periphery of last night.

His chill thaws for a split second. "Ah, Tootsie. I'm sorry. I'm sorry about your pain. *Mais, tu sais, l'amour, c'est banale et unique.*" He tosses this off as if he's throwing a handful of salt over his shoulder.

"THAT'S YOUR ADVICE?" My head becomes encased

in a helmet of mercury. Why is he always saying this shit while I'm driving?

My father goes back to staring out the window.

In a final, futile, demented attempt to calm myself, I do an inventory of people I would rather be on this trip with. It is longer than all the other lists I've made on this trip. Longer than the wine-name lists, the drink lists, the pain inventory lists, the lists of facts I've learned about his history. All of them.

My father navigates us to the Château de la Tuilerie using two fingers and monosyllables. I park. Our two-man funeral procession enters the main building. My father announces our arrival to a man with gray hair and stunning body odor. The man replies that Chantal Comte is on her way. We thank him like a couple of strangers who have arrived early for a job interview in a factory.

I turn my back to my father and scan the walls. I make the Face of Intense Contemplation.

I turn around only when Chantal Comte sweeps into the tasting salon. Chantal Comte seems to be the type of woman who sweeps into every room she enters. She is a woman built for sweeping and dresses herself in clothes that have a high sweep factor. Surely she has paid a good deal of money for the fancy outfit she is wearing, but she is a Rubenesque woman, so it really just looks like a bias-cut designer muumuu. Her hair is brown and thick and glossy. She approaches my father and me, smiling vaguely, businesslike, arm outstretched but with a limp wrist, the way high society ladies do. She doesn't look like any of the other vintners we've met. It is harvest season, her hands should be stained black from the skins of the grapes. She should be wearing boots and smelling of the sun and of dirt. But she smells of expensive perfume. Perfume! No one puts on perfume in the morning when they know they'll be tasting wine! Even *I* know that, and I know nothing! How am I going to be able to smell her wine with that expensive perfume getting in the way?

I did not like Mme. Nudant, but I do not buy Chantal Comte.

My father has plenty of experience with women like this. He has dealt with seven hundred thousand Chantal Comtes in his life. Chantal Comtes love my father, because he is handsome and charming without being sleazy at all. He softens his eyes for them, and he asks them probing questions—but not too probing—insightful, interested questions, with eyebrows arched and mouth parted in anticipation. Then, when the Chantal Comtes are responding, he cocks his head at a perfect angle, which makes them believe the entire universe has ceased to exist, and they are now alone, just two people, floating on some parallel plane, and only Chantal Comte is talking and only my father is listening and it is so, so, *so* special.

"*Bonjour, madame. Enchanté. Philippe Borel. Ma fille, Kathryn Borel.*" He smiles a small, elegant smile.

"*Monsieur. Mademoiselle. Bienvenue,*" she responds.

Chantal Comte is running an empire, she is a busy woman,

she has meetings, one that is in a few short hours, we must get down to it, and soon enough we are sitting on curly, ornate metal stools around a small marble-topped island in the middle of the salon. There is a copper sink carved into the marble, for spitting.

She summons Yves, the salon's sommelier, to open five bottles of wine. The convergence of the smells destroys my last minuscule hope that I might extract some secret private joy out of this experience.

My father is asking the appropriate questions, he is being so gracious, are the oak barrels new or old, what qualities have they given the wine, oh, this one is called Un Des Sens, what a clever name, how did you come up with such a witty double entendre, one of the senses/indecency, oh ha ha, tell me about this year's harvest, would you like to hear a clever quote by a famous writer, because I would like to tell you this clever quote by a famous writer.

Chantal Comte and my father are laughing. I am seething.

"You know, Madame Comte, we've been traveling for a week and a half now and I still don't know how to spit properly. When I do, it dribbles down my chin," I say sweetly.

I plant my splayed hand on the bottom of the glass to do a proper swirl. The glass scrapes and screeches on the marble. My father and Chantal Comte cringe. I stick my nose into the glass, inhale deeply, then drink, making the appropriate kissing noises to run the liquid over my tongue. Mouth facing the sink, I spit. The wine sprays outward, a flat wet red triangle, all over the counter, my sleeves, and my father's sleeves. Some goes into the sink. But not much.

"Do you see?" I say. "My father, however, is the champion of spitting! We've met many sommeliers, and many wine-makers, and none of them spit as gracefully and stylishly as *mon papa*! When the wine comes out of his mouth, it's like a laser!"

Mme. Comte shoots me a look of distaste and reengages my father, who has turned his head away from me. *If you want me to be a child, Dad, if being a child is the only way we can relate . . . then I will be a child for you.*

We continue the tasting. I hear the words. I drink the wine. Château de la Tuilerie, 2004. Accolades, 2004, made, I think, with Alicante. Alicante? This is a new grape. *You are being a grouchy asshole.* Château de la Tuilerie, Carte Blanche, 2004. Syrah and Grenache. Grapes I know from the region. The wind cleans the grapes. I know this. *Maybe you should start trying again.* Château de la Tuilerie Cuvée Éole Rouge, 2001. An older wine. But not so old. Un Des Sens, 2003. Made only with Syrah. Chantal Comte and my father chat. They chat and chat. They laugh more. *No, fuck trying. You've been trying the whole time. He's the one who hasn't been trying with you. You learned the language pretty well, for a while. It's he who hasn't bothered to learn yours.* I look down at my boots to hide the fact that my eyes are brimming with tears. Several minutes pass.

I am still looking at my boots when a different smell, one that's astringent and nauseatingly familiar, wafts into my face.

"Tou Tou. Taste Madame Comte's rum. It's from Antilles," my father says. He says this for her benefit, not mine.

Rum. Christ. Anything but rum. Red wine over rum. I take it all back. I can't taste the rum. I suppress a burp. Somewhere along the tube of my esophagus there's a gurgling sting.

"Oh, non, merci, madame . . . mais . . ." There's no chance of my finishing the sentence. I have been avoiding rum like rats and ebola since I was seventeen, after the Night of my First—sorry, Second—Poisoning, a night that left me spent and sick in a hotel bathroom, a night that involved me sleeping in a pool of my own vomit. Rum is the stuff of my nightmares.

They are laughing again, Yves is taking away the balloon glasses, their rims stained burgundy and smeared with saliva and lipstick. He leaves. It is an orgy of smell.

Rising, I excuse myself from the table, then march quickly through the salon and into the storage area where the bathroom is. I lock the door and drop to my knees, heaving into the toilet, exhaling in one long, red stream all of Chantal Comte's wine, her perfume, their laughter, which I can still hear, floating under the closed door. All of it.

chapter thirteen

The car is no longer a car. It is a clear Lucite box that only a contortionist could bend into. But we have both somehow found ourselves crammed into it. I am driving west, but there is nowhere to go. The air is like soup. Something— some reflex—I don't know, I don't know if it's a reflex, but it is something . . . something is blocking this air from finding a settling place in my lungs. I can't breathe in fully. I have no tools.

After leaving Chantal Comte's château, we spend an endless amount of our (now separate) futures winding along roads, making wrong turns, becoming lost in a field where there are vines and then, later, goats. We are back at the beginning of the trip. The difference is that he no longer feels like my father. He feels like a stranger. And I refuse to register what he is experiencing. That is no longer my solemn duty.

The large converted barn doors of the small hotel we're meant to be staying at are barricaded. My father has exited the car and returned with the note that was taped to the wood. It reads, *"Au marché. Retour: 17h."* The owners will be returning at five p.m. It is two p.m. My spirits sink lower. I want to eat by myself and lock myself into my room for the rest of the day. As we were getting lost, I resolved that I would call my mother from the privacy of my hotel room, explain the situation, describe how my father was acting in plain terms, allow her to understand the impact it was having on me, and ask her to help bring me home. All I need is a hotel room, some safe distance away from him.

"I'm not waiting here," I say.

Map in lap, my father points to the nearest city, Alès. I wind back down the road and follow the signs.

Without exchanging a word, we drive for another few hundred years. Pastoral village turns into gray industry— stores, neon green *pharmacie* crosses every few blocks, a City Hall made of stone. Noticing a red panel on one of the pointed green road signs, I make out the familiar icon of two red flowers, Ibis Centr'Ales. It's the French equivalent to a Holiday Inn. *This will do.*

I lock the car and throw the keys in the direction of my father's chest, trying to hit the red knighthood stripe he has pinned to this blazer. *What a joke.* After almost ten years of what was said to be unparalleled leadership at the Château Frontenac, his work was noticed by the French government, and in 2001 he received the Chevalier de la Légion d'honneur designation, France's equivalent of knighthood. I throw the keys at him as hard as I can. I want to knock off his dumb little red stripe. I miss his chest, he misses the keys, then picks them up as I walk ahead to make reservation and check-in arrangements. He's not far behind. We arrive at the desk together. It appears as though Alès is in the midst of some sort of festival. The young woman at the desk is wearing a billowy, humiliating period costume.

She hands us the keys to our separate bedrooms, on separate floors. I am hit by a typhoon of relief. Distance from him. Now I can make the phone call.

In the elevator, I press 3 and he presses 5. The doors open, I get out. He follows.

No.

No, goddammit.

I whirl around. "What are you doing?" I demand.

He shrugs and wrinkles up his face. He's conceding something in this shrug, in this expression.

"*Eh,* well, Tootsie, you know, I just . . . I just . . . wanted to check to see how crappy this room is."

"No. Leave me alone."

"Okay, Tou Tou." He turns and moves back toward the elevator. Before continuing the walk down the hall, I make sure he enters it. I watch his face disappear as the metal doors slide shut.

I slip the key card in and out. There is suction as I push the door in. The room isn't bad. It smells a bit of cigarette smoke. Sitting down slowly on the bed, I realize I am completely worn out. I unzip my boots and throw them in the corner. I shift into a supine position and close my eyes. I pass out immediately.

It is early evening when I wake up. I am hollow and hungry, and I have to take a piss. After flipping on the light on the bedside table, I scan the room. My bag, which contains the phone, is by the door to the room. Next to it, there's a piece of hotel stationery, folded in half. I can suddenly feel all the muscles in my body. I walk over and pick up the note, unfold it, and read my father's flat, near illegible script.

My Dear Tou Tou,

You were right. There are ways in which I really have failed you. Last night I did not know what to do. You were throwing so many emotions at me—this is not bad, really! This is good! I need to know these parts of you. You were telling the truth about you, and I did not respond. I have not killed that mean man you saw in the car last night, and today, but I have banished him to another planet. Please come and talk to me when you can. I promise I will listen to you. I can see you are becoming a girl of real weight. You know what I mean—Beethoven moving from his first to his second period.

Love,

Dad

I blink at the page and see that I've left impression marks on the sides of the page, from where my now moist, clammy fingers have been clamped.

In my stocking feet, I walk down the hall, achy and stiff from the nap, carrying in my gut a good, anticipatory warmth. I trust these words. I take the stairs to the fifth floor.

"Hi." I'm standing in the doorway.

"Tootsie."

He invites me in.

"I took a nap. I needed some sleep."

"Good."

"Thank you for writing that note."

"Bah." He squeezes his shoulders into a sheepish mea culpa shrug. "You're welcome."

"You know, I was going to leave today. I was going to find some way to leave you," I say.

He opens his arms. I walk over and let myself be folded within them. My eyes well up and my nose begins to run. Running my face back and forth on his sweater, I wipe my face clean, leaving a trail of snot and tears. Putting his hands on my shoulders, he pushes me back gently and notices the mess.

"Thank you for this gift of your *morve*."

"You're welcome. For the snot. And the rest. It's the least I can do—your note was pretty great."

"*Alors, on va manger?*" Yes. *We will eat.*

"Yes."

"*Et, le champagne?*"

"Yes."

As we walk into the street, the day is new. The sky has

changed colors—a rainstorm has just passed through. The city looks better, cleaner. My dad chuckles and pokes his finger up at the sky.

There's a huge rainbow. A huge, seriously huge, and hugely cheerful rainbow. I buckle and flop over, in hysterics. I shake my fist at the rainbow.

"Our lives are a cliché," my dad says.

chapter fourteen

My father's fork hovers over my clam pasta. Repositioning my own so the prongs are aimed at him, I let the fork slice through the air sideways. The two pieces of metal make a clanging noise and his fork flies out of his hand and onto the floor. He raises his eyebrows and smiles. I lean over, pick it up, make a show out of cleaning it with my napkin—breathing on it and wiping it down—and hand it back to him.

"Do you want to make a deal with me?" I ask.

"Sure."

"When you want some of my food, ask me first. You know, instead of just helping yourself."

"Deal. Hey, Toots."

"Yes, Dad."

"Give me some of your pasta?"

I push my plate closer to him.

"Hey, Toots."

"Yes?"

"Can I tell you a story about me?"

"Of course."

"I don't know—this story might not move you in any way . . ." He hesitates. "But maybe it will explain to you why I act strange sometimes. I don't know. Maybe not."

He swallows a sip of his champagne. "So, in the spring, in 1965, I was living in Montreal. In a very small apartment."

"That was when you were working for the airline, peddling gourmet food to the drunken bloaters on the plane." I pluck a gray clamshell from the tangle and perch it on the tip of my nose. "Continue, please," I say gravely.

"Yes." He takes note of the clam but continues without laughing, "I was woken up in the middle of the night by a lot of loud banging outside my door. There was banging and yelling—a big noise. I went to my door to check out what was happening. When I opened the door, there were men standing there. In police uniforms. They came into my *leetle* apartment and threw me against the wall, then let me go, then told me to put some clothes on." My father is speaking in an eerie calm voice.

"What—why was this happening?" I remove the clamshell from my nose and place it slowly back onto the plate.

"I'm getting there, Toots. Stay with me. The story is a bit long. The men said I had five minutes. While I put on my pants and jacket, they walked around my apartment and knocked things over. They made a mess of everything. I was thrown in a car and taken to a room in the police station. It was a gray room. I sat there for a long time. Probably a few hours. There were no windows in the room, so I didn't know what time it was or how long I'd been sitting there."

"You're burying the lead, Dad. What was *happening*?" I repeat, suddenly anxious.

"I had been arrested, with a group of my colleagues, in a huge heroin bust."

I stare at him, perplexed. *How is this only coming out now?* A piece of pasta dislodges itself from my molar and catches in the back of my throat. I cough into my napkin.

"For three days, three police worked in shifts, interrogating me. One detective with the Royal Mounted Police, one from the FBI, one agent with Interpol. They questioned me for hours and hours. They threatened me, insulted me. Then they would stop and become gentle. They were empathetic, understanding. And then they would turn it around again. Bigger threats, more violence. Sometimes they would stop and put me back in my cage so that I could sleep for fifteen minutes." Now he is punching his words. He grabs his glass of champagne so that the liquid sloshes around. I want to tell him to put it down, to wait until the end of his story.

"This sounds like a cop movie," I say.

"Like in the fucking most predictable cop movie you've ever seen," he spits.

"What did you do? What did you say to them? What did they say to you?"

"Nothing, Toots. I did nothing. I said nothing to them.

I stayed on my little chair and kept quiet. I went to another place. I disappeared in front of their eyes. I was still very young—I was just twenty-six. You know what it is like to have an *experience déterminante*—a bad one—when you are so young."

I move my head up and down. "You have to keep going with the story."

"At the end of three days, the cops were very frustrated with me. The one from Interpol—he was a short man from France—put his hand on my shoulder and said in my ear, *'Des petits mecs comme vous, tout ce que ça merite c'est douze balles dans le dos.'* "

"All you deserve is twelve bullets in the back . . ."

"Yes."

"What were you accused of, exactly?"

"There were three crimes: illegally importing drugs, trafficking, and being a member of a drug ring. Each charge was a minimum of seven years in prison. The operative word, of course, was 'minimum.' "

"But they were just accusations . . . And you didn't admit anything . . ."

"I said nothing to them. I did not 'admit' because I had nothing to admit to. It was not my story. When they put me back in the holding cell—my cage—I thought about Sugar Ray Robinson and Jake LaMotta. During their sixth fight— their final fight—Sugar Ray had Jake up against the ropes. Jake's face looked like pudding, totally deformed. His eyes were so fat they were only *sleets*. He had his arms up and

Sugar Ray was raining punches on him. The referee stopped the fight and raised Sugar Ray's hand above his head. He was the new middleweight champion of the world. Everyone was cheering. But then Jake walked over to Sugar Ray. He looked at him with his poor broken face and said, 'You couldn't knock me out, Sugar Ray, you couldn't knock me out.'"

"And so?" Under the table, I am tearing a cardboard coaster into one million pieces. *He didn't get knocked out, though. Neither did I.*

"And so I had my first van ride, in handcuffs. And my first cavity search. And my first tiny penitentiary cell at Bordeaux prison. It had dirty walls and a bed that was all caved in. It was the first time I felt massive contempt for humankind."

"But you didn't do anything WRONG."

"Ah, yes, but that was not the point. I was accused. If I remember correctly, something like ten other men were accused with me. Everyone was interrogated. One man had accused me. He was covering for someone. Who? We'll never know."

"You were accused by only one man. So you went to jail anyway."

"Yes."

"What about your lawyer?"

"I had one. He was bad. Incompetent. He did not believe my story."

"And you lost."

"I lost, and they threw me in the slammer." He pronounces it *slah-MURR.*

All at once, I notice how screwy my face feels. Rage has settled in my cheeks, drawing them up, causing my eyes to squint. My jaw has tightened, causing my mouth to gape. I smooth my hand over my bangs and down, grazing my nose and chin. *He was twenty-six and he was in jail. I am twenty-six and I'm on a wine trip.*

"Keep going."

"Well, you know. I adapted. If I stood on my toes and grabbed on to the bars of the window in my cell, I could lift myself up and see some sky. But there were awful things in there. I saw a man get stabbed in the line for lunch one day—with a spoon that had been shaped into a sharp point. So I shut my mouth. I shut my mouth and went along with the routines."

"How long were you there?"

"At the beginning, I did not think I'd be there for long. But after the terrible lawyer, and so much bad luck, and the injustice, I had no idea. About anything. Toots, I had no *idea*. At one point, I had to start to believe that I'd be there for the full sentence. I had to move on."

"Move on from WHAT?"

"Just move on from the idea of being free."

"Oh, Dad." I reach across my plate and tap my index finger to the back of his hand. My eyes become teary.

"There were weeks when I would not have one conversation. For a little while, at the beginning, I developed a relationship with the man in the cell next door. My neighbor was a municipal worker—and member of the Front de libération du Québec. He had been convicted of making homemade bombs and dropping them in Canada Post boxes. This lasted for a little while. But he could not endure it. On the Sunday before Easter, he'd been very upset. He missed his wife and his two daughters. So on Easter Monday, he used the leather strap he needed to hold his wooden leg in place . . . and hung himself with it."

My gaze drops slightly and stops at my father's neck. I watch his Adam's apple pop in and out as he swallows another mouthful of his champagne.

"Did you think about suicide?" I ask him this in my quietest voice.

His face becomes stern. It is the same face of the man who held me by the shoulders in that summer of 2001 while I cried and fretted over a meal of orzo.

"It almost *keeled* me . . . ," he says.

But your life is no longer your own once you are loved. Something inside me solidifies. *I have the courage to be accountable to the people I love. His parents were waiting on the outside of the disaster, helping when they could. Mine had done the same, in their way.*

I stop picking at my leftover clams. They are too cold to eat. Instead, I place my fork next to my plate, grab the edge of the table with both hands, and squeeze it.

"You have to tell me how you got out, now," I demand.

"My mother saved me. And luck, I guess. My mother found a very good attorney—a man named Jacques Bédard. The trial began. Every other week, I sat in front of an elderly judge. He had no time for me or the defense. Every month, Bédard would put in a bail request with him. It was rejected over and over again. But then, in the summer—the late summer—there was a new judge who was called to do the bail hearings. His name was Larose. Larose and Bédard were friends from childhood. Larose trusted Bédard. My bail was set at twenty thousand dollars. A friend of the family, a dentist, Dr. Capelle, wrote the check. He signed over the title to his house as a guarantee to the bank. I left prison after being there for almost six months. In June of the following year, the two others were sentenced to ten and fifteen years in prison. And in October 1966, I was acquitted."

We look at each other for a while. I smooth out the napkin sitting on my lap. He pinches several *frites allumettes*, squashes them together so they're a squashy potato mass, dips them in mayonnaise, and crams his fingers in his mouth. Walking my fingers over to his plate, I mimic him. I swallow and run my tongue around my mouth to taste the residual starch and salt.

"Dad."

"What is it?"

"You were innocent, right?"

"What do you think?"

"I think yes."

"I guess I am the only person who will ever know."

"Come on, Dad."

"Yes, yes. Yes, Tootsen. I was. It was my great test. I came through. I did not fold. My innocence carried me through. It enabled me to deal with whatever life threw at me for all of it—for the rest of my *life*." He slams his hand on the table with anger or defiance or both. Our glasses wobble.

I pause and think about this.

"I wish you had told me that story earlier. I wish I could have known that about you . . ." I waver for a moment. *Would it have really helped to know this about him last year, two years ago, four years ago?* "It maybe would have helped me make sense of some of the things about you that scare me. That make me nuts. I could have at least understood a little more about the place you go when you get quiet. That it is not about you rejecting me. You not loving me."

"Of course it is not about that!"

"But, the accident . . . the way it affects my decisions, my behavior . . . it would have been nice to know about that piece of you so that I could have deciphered your language a little better. We could have maybe compared notes . . ." I trail off. *His story isn't the Answer. But it is one important variable in a big pile of other variables. It's like knowing whether he had a rainy or a dry October.*

"But now you know. You know some of my ghosts," he says.

"Yes."

"And I know some of your ghosts."

"The accident?"

"Not the accident—but what it has done to you. Your accident has made you afraid of endings, Toots. I see that now. When I disappear in front of you, or when I become a crazy person, you are watching the end of the man you know."

He's dying a little death every day. At least you know a little more about the he who is dying. I shudder a bit, then stop.

"I am a lucky guy," he says.

"Sure, I guess . . ."

"No, I am a lucky guy. Because you are brave and patient."

"Thank you." I reach across the table and with a clumsy hand cup his cheek and give him a few avuncular pats—which are really more like slaps—and joke, "See, Dad, we *did* get to go to Bordeaux on this trip. Sort of."

"Fuck Bordeaux," he says, and laughs.

"Yeah, fuck that place," I say back to him.

We weave through the narrow streets of Alès, all of which are jammed with revelers for some festival that is obviously about to begin. They jostle us as we force our way through what is becoming a standard small-city mob scene, full of awkward, thick-lipped teens looking for make-out partners and tacky forty-year-old couples with thinner lips who are nevertheless dressed like the thick-lipped teens. On another night, on a night like two nights ago, my father would have been cursing and lamenting his poor knee, his poor knee, and I would have been frantically making the peace. But tonight we have opened our Cracker Jack boxes and traded decoder rings. We navigate the crowd without needing to say a word, for once.

Before climbing into bed, I stand barefoot on the clammy, smoky hotel rug, catching the faraway party sounds in my ears and rising street smells in my nose. Then, a popping, like a gunshot. *PAF!* My heart beats fast and the space behind my eyes grows tingly with panic, until I notice the lion's mane of gold glitter in the sky. For a while I look at the fireworks, think a little about destruction and creation, then leave the window to watch *Top Gear* on the BBC World Service.

chapter fifteen

I push at the tacky dark green and dirty gold comforter and breathe in the manky hotel room air. I kick up my legs so the leaden thing pops off my body, then parachutes around me, landing with as much of a thud as a comforter can make. It is a combination of a poof and a thud. I do it a second time, but this time I punt both legs simultaneously to the left. The movement works. The comforter sails off my body and I look down at my crisp sheet-swathed body and feel a swell of relief: It is our last day on the road. And then I get up like girls do in Disney movies, all precious and motivated, waiting for the little birds to come and help them get dressed.

I take a very hot shower and then a very cold shower, use the hair dryer, put clothing on, and take the elevator downstairs to my dad's room. Predicting my arrival, he has wedged a folded room service menu between the locking mechanism and the door frame. I enter, letting the door click shut behind me. The room smells of soap, the bathroom door is open.

"Are you decent?" I call.

"Yes, yes, Tootsie. My Tou Tou. Come in."

I peer around the corner to find my dad with a towel around his waist and a look of utter rapture on his face. In his ear, a Q-tips. He's rotating it around, slowly, counterclockwise.

"There you go, doing that," I say.

"What?" he asks.

"What you do with your Q-tips. Your rapturous exercise of cleaning your ears. I know how much you love cleaning your ears. I love it, too."

"It is like sex without the effort."

The room service menu is in my hand. Flicking my wrist hard, I send it sailing into the bathroom. It rotates fast—the corner hits my father on the right part of his rib cage and leaves a mark.

"Owwsh!"

"You say gross, horrible things, and you must be punished for them."

"That is fair."

He finishes his ear excavation and puts the used Q-tips back in his shaving kit.

As we drive into the courtyard of our final stop, Clos Bagatelle, I think about his lecture to me on the day before we boarded the plane. The day that now feels like thou-

sands of millions of years away. He talked about Languedoc
and the new identity of the region. He said the winemakers
here had not recognized the raw material they had under
and all around them. How their wines had been blunt and
lacking complexity—stuff that was meant to be drunk
pragmatically—to quench thirst, maybe render one intoxicated. And now the region was being blessed, for the first
time since the identity shift, with a legendary vintage.

The Clos Bagatelle winery is paradisiacal. The color palette knows no pastels. It is fiery red earth and cyan sky, the
vivid green of the vines and the mushroom gill brown of the
surrounding bluffs.

Two wiry German shepherd teen dogs bound toward
us, barking their heads off. They trot around us in a circle,
round and round, wet noses poking our thighs.

"Bonjour, les chiens." My father lets them sniff him all
over.

I stroke one of them between the eyes.

An angular woman with a tomboyish haircut and sparkly
eyes hurries out the stone house at the end of the drive. She's
in jeans and a big knit white sweater and approaches us, waving with both arms as though she's standing outside a gate at
the airport and we're family members getting off the plane.
Grabbing my father's hand with her right and enclosing both
hands with her left, she shakes the mess of fingers and palms
enthusiastically. She turns to me and brings me in for *la bise.*
I air-kiss her cheeks and giggle, dumbfounded but mostly
charmed. It's as though scientists created an antithetical clon-

ing machine and put Chantal Comte in it, then transplanted the result to this vineyard in Saint-Chinian. Her name is Christine Simon. Clos Bagatelle belongs to her.

"Did you get lost?"

"No, amazingly," I respond.

"Amazingly?" This woman cares about my qualification. I become flustered.

"Oh. Yes. I mean, amazingly, because we've been getting lost a lot. You're our last stop on what's been a long trip."

She eyes my father, grinning. "You've been trapped in the car with each other for how long?"

"Environs deux semaines," my father says.

"Two weeks!"

"More than a thousand kilometers," I say.

"And you haven't killed each other yet?"

"Almost," I say. The image of the tree scrolls by. I giggle again, through tight lips. The result sounds like a combination of a toad and a bird's mating call.

"Bien fait!" she congratulates me, and slaps my arm. "So, you're tired of tours, I assume. I'll take you around. We'll make it quick. And then, *une jolie dégustation*." This woman reads minds.

Walking briskly, dogs in tow, she gives us the movie trailer tour. Old family-owned property, old vines, old casks. Thirty-nine hectares. Red grapes: Syrah, Grenache, Mourvedre, Carignan. They plop in some white grapes when making red wines, a smattering of Muscat mixed with the Mourvedre; Viognier with the Syrah. Many of the wines are named after family members: Camille, Juliette. She stops and turns, her eyes scanning ours.

"Our best wine is called La Gloire de Mon Père," she says. The Glory of My Father. It's the title of a Marcel Pagnol book I read when I was a child. "My brother and I dedicated our top cuvée to our father, Henry. He died seven years ago."

I nod. My father nods. She nods.

"*A table!*" she says, and marches off in the direction of the tasting room. We follow. My dad looks amused.

"*What?*" I whisper.

"*Eet's* nothing," he says.

"Come on, *what?*"

"She is a good daughter, to make a wine for her father. You too are a good daughter, but how are you going to honor me when I am dead in the ground?"

"First, I will take you to a taxidermist and have you stuffed like a sailfish. Then, I'll have your joints replaced with nuts and bolts so that on weekends I can turn my living room into a theater and make you perform humiliating dance routines in front of all the people who once respected you," I whisper back to him, slowly and methodically, wearing my creepiest smile.

"HA!" He reaches out and squeezes my shoulder.

"You asked."

At the table, which is heavy and thick, sit three people who are ready to drink. Christine is Inspector Gadget, with a corkscrew thrusting out the sleeve of her sweater, opening bottles and bottles and bottles, introducing them into the group while letting us continue to introduce ourselves.

"Who's the expert here?" she asks.

My dad and I both point to each other. I take his index finger in my hand and I fold it back into his fist.

"It's my father," I say. "I've been trying to learn."

"And? What have you learned?"

"The list is long."

"Well?" She swirls and sips one of her 2002 vintages. My father and I do the same. I look into the glass and allow some air to roll into my mouth. The flavor expands—it blooms into prunes and cloves.

"Well, mostly I figured out that it's impossible to force a connection—that sometimes, if I'm not in the right mood, no matter how great the wine is, there's very little chance that it'll have any impact."

"Good answer."

"I also learned that it's important that I learn how to spit properly. Watch this," I say, pulling in the spittoon. I hold my head over the opening and dribble a mouthful of wine into it. This time, the liquid runs not only down my chin, but down my neck and into my cleavage. I dab at the mess with the sleeve of my sweater. My father cackles into his knees. Christine touches my wrist and spits, sending a perfect jet of wine into the receptacle.

"Make a little fish face, like this," she says, puckering her lips and making her cheeks go concave. "Next, you want to push your tongue against your top two teeth, then widen it out so that it's touching all the teeth in the top row."

"Okay."

"Now try." She hands me a glass.

I expel the wine with as much technique and gusto as I can. The first half jets out cleverly, the rest finds its way into my shirt.

"Presque!" Christine says, applauding.

"Almost there, Toots." My father pats my knee.

A group of Austrian tourists bursts into the room, interrupting our moment with loud questions about the price of the rosé. Christine's brother Luc appears, deals with their queries, and ushers them out. We make fun of their ridiculous hats and sense of entitlement. And oh, my God, do we ever laugh. At the Austrians, at everything. But especially at the Austrians and their Tyrolean hats with feathers and cords. We're having a party.

Before we leave, Christine gives us a bottle of Henry's wine. On the label, she writes two words: *"Moment magique."*

It takes us a day and a half to get back to Paris. We retrace our steps almost exactly, even staying over in the same hotel in Burgundy. We drive up, up, up, until we get to the middle of the top of France. Driving toward the *centre-ville* gives me the type of feeling I imagine Olympians have when they're sitting in crisp suits in convertible cars and the sky is raining confetti. I am a float of myself in the Macy's Thanksgiving Day parade. I am one thousand feet tall and so shiny, and I can shoot heart-shaped lasers out of my eyes and wine out of my mouth like a semipro. Though apparently I'm still useless at following road signs, as we get lost while trying to find the Gare de Lyon, where we're meant to drop off the rental car.

In the underground parking lot that smells of urine and trains, my father steps out of our home-on-wheels for the last time. He says he needs to do a big stretch.

With his hands on his hips, he arches his back. Without looking at me, he says, "Tootsie, make sure the car *eez* clean." His tone indicates he will be taking no part in this cleaning.

"Sure thing." I find a flimsy gas station plastic bag and begin pinching up the garbage. Bits of soft old Kleenex and dirty pipe cleaners and ink-smeared receipts. Plastic Nescafé cups and one hair elastic. A cork, a different type of cup. I go through the backseat pockets and into the inset rubber troughs attached to the bottoms of the car doors. More receipts, a package of plastic-wrapped hotel Q-tips. There are three, and they are clean. I put them in my satchel. There is some loose change, grit, and dust. I find two wrinkled Michelin maps of France. One has been folded properly, the other not. I attack the backseat. We've amassed a collection of gift bottles from everyone: Rémy Gresser, Manou Massenez, Bernard Nast, Marie-Anne Nudant, René Aubert, Chantal Comte, Christine Simon. I take care in rolling each in my sweaters and pants, placing the wine-clothing sausages into my backpack, releasing the plastic clasps and the nylon straps to accommodate them. I throw my father's untied running shoes into his big rectangular megabriefcase, as well as the navy blue briefs that are hanging to dry on the car coat hanger by the back passenger window. I do a final sweep. I pop open the glove compartment. There is a third Michelin map of France and the vinegar book.

Outside the window, I catch a glimpse of my father. He has completed his stretching routine and is now quizzically flipping through his Day-Timer, checking that all his ID and credit cards are in there. He snaps closed the leather cover and in a loud voice says, "So. Tootsie. Let's get this show on the road, *hein?*"

"You are a show," I say.

"No, *you* are a show," he says.

I haul out our things and and lock the car. I pile all the trip viscera next to a tire and stare at it. We hear footsteps coming toward us, echoing ominously against the pillars and low concrete ceiling. My father turns in the direction of the footsteps. I do, too. A priest is walking toward us in full black robes, his hands clasped behind his back. He has a little blond mustache and is wearing black sneakers. My dad gawks openly at him as he sweeps by us. It's embarrassing—so I reach out and pull out one of his ear hairs. Wincing in pain, he reflexively reels around and smacks me in the bicep.

"That *hurt*," he cries.

I rub my bicep. "I wanted you to stop staring at that man!"

"Sorry."

"It's all right."

"He looked like a pedophile, don't you think?"

I crinkle my nose at my father, then adjust the angle of my head so that I can see over my father's shoulder. The priest's robe is swishing stiffly, left and right. A tuft of blond neck hair sprouts out of the back of his collar. I look back at him.

"I love you. Even though you look like a pedophile. That's why God hates you so much," I say in my darlingest voice.

"Well, it makes sense. Daughter loves her pedophile-looking dad. That's why God hates *you* so much."

"We have that much in common."

"At least, Toots. At *least*."